THE SECRET OF SPIRITUAL JOY

William P. Farley
Cruciform Press | November 2015

To Sarah Jones, Anne Nelson,
Ruth Hisaw, David Farley,
and Joseph Farley.

May I leave you, my children,
a legacy of gratitude.

– Bill Farley

Cruciform Press

"One always reads 'the secret of…' with some degree of incredulity. Is there really one thing, above all else, that can be demonstrated to be *the* secret? In this instance Bill Farley has made his case and it is compelling. Oh, what biblical wisdom is contained in this brief book, wrapped in engrossing historical and contemporaries stories that illustrate beautifully the richness of that biblical truth. Reading this book has given me greater earnestness to pursue the path of joy Farley has here mapped so skillfully. May God be pleased to use this book to do the same for innumerable other Christian pilgrims."

Bruce A. Ware, author; Chairman, Department of Christian Theology, The Southern Baptist Theological Seminary

"Continuing his explorations of how the biblical gospel both fuels and shapes the cultivation of Christ-like virtues, Bill Farley turns his attention in this volume to the joy that sadly seems to elude so many believers. I especially appreciate how he interweaves solid theology with practical illustrations so that all who read this short but powerful book can emerge with a trustworthy and clear understanding of how to recognize and experience this gracious blessing from the Lord."

Randal Roberts, President and Professor of Spiritual Formation, Western Seminary

"Relentless thanksgiving…exuberant gratitude…absolute sovereignty…the cross of Jesus Christ. All of these converge (rightly so!) in this brief pastoral piece by Bill Farley. Moreover, they do so with the intention of obliterating our propensities for grumbling and self-pity. This may prove to be a dangerous book for those who wallow in dispositions that are antithetical to the Christian gospel."

Art Azurdia, Senior Minister of Word and Worship at Trinity Church (Portland, OR); Director, Doctor of Ministry Program, Western Seminary

Table of Contents

Cruciform Press

Books of about 100 pages
Clear, inspiring, gospel-centered
CruciformPress.com

We like to keep it simple. So we publish short, clear, useful, inexpensive books for Christians and other curious people. Books that make sense and are easy to read, even as they tackle serious subjects.

We do this because the good news of Jesus Christ—the gospel—is the only thing that actually explains why this world is so wonderful and so awful all at the same time. Even better, the gospel applies to every single area of life, and offers real answers that aren't available from any other source.

These are books you can afford, enjoy, finish easily, benefit from, and remember. Check us out and see. Then join us as part of a publishing revolution that's good news for the gospel, the church, and the world.

The Secret of Spiritual Joy

Print / PDF ISBN: 978-1-941114-14-8
Epub ISBN: 978-1-941114-16-2
Mobipocket ISBN: 978-1-941114-15-5

INTRODUCTION

If *The Secret of Spiritual Joy* sounds like a pretentious title, I don't mean it that way. This book is not a cure for all that ails us, a guarantee of cork-popping effervescence for the rest of your life. It is about the application of a crucial biblical principle that if applied methodically will increase your faith, amplify your humility, and expand your joy.

I have intentionally not titled it *The Secret of Spiritual Happiness.* We generally become happy when we interpret external circumstances as good or positive. When the weather is nice and everyone loves me I *feel* happy. But happiness is not a common biblical idea. The English Standard Version of the Bible translates the original languages into *happy* or *happiness* only thirteen times. By contrast, *joy*, *rejoice*, or *joyful* appear 359 times.

Joy is something we are commanded to do. It is also something we experience. It is a fruit of the Spirit. Like happiness, joy can refer to positive feelings flowing from pleasant circumstances. But it can also refer to a deep-down-inside, quiet, settled conviction that all is well even when circumstances are horrendous.

For example, James exhorts us to "count it all joy…when you meet trials of various kinds" (James 1:2). And Paul describes himself as "sorrowful, yet always rejoicing" (2 Corinthians 6:10). Then, in the next chapter, he describes himself as in "affliction" yet "overflowing with joy" (2 Corinthians 7:4). The words *trials*, *sorrowful*, and *affliction* don't normally go with rejoicing and joy, but for those who apply the contents of this book they will be more and more intimately entwined. "For the joy that was set before him [Jesus] endured the cross" (Hebrews 12:2).

In other words, by faith every believer can access spiritual joy even when life is serving up occasions for sorrow. I am not talking about a simplistic cure-all for a miserable day, the escape from sorrow at a loved one's death, or a quick fix for the discouragement produced by a lost job. I am talking about a faith response which, despite miserable circumstances, says at the heart level: all is well with my soul.

Horatio Spafford (1828–1888) knew this joy in seriously adverse circumstances. In 1870 his only son died of scarlet fever. Then in 1871 the great Chicago fire destroyed much of his wealth. A few months later, Spafford sent his wife and four daughters ahead of him to Europe while he stayed in Chicago to wrap up some business affairs. The ship carrying his family collided with another vessel and sank. All four daughters died. Only his wife, Anna, survived. From Europe she telegraphed her husband these dismal words, "Saved alone!" Grief-stricken, Spafford quickly sailed for Europe to comfort his grieving wife. As his ship passed the area where his four daughters had drowned he penned the lyrics to the famous hymn, *It is Well with My Soul.* The first verse captures the essence of spiritual joy.

> When peace like a river, attendeth my way,
> When sorrows like sea billows roll;
> Whatever my lot, Thou hast taught me to say,
> It is well, it is well, with my soul.

Despite sorrows that seemed to roll on endlessly, Spafford knew what the apostle Paul called the "peace of God, which surpasses all understanding" (Philippians 4:7). This is a deep, quiet confidence in three things.

- First, that God loves me, has everything under control, and works all of life's events together for my good and the good of all those who love him.
- Second, that I deserve much worse than I am getting, but because of the cross I will never get it.
- Third, "joy that is inexpressible and filled with glory" (1 Peter 1:8), "the peace of God, which surpasses all understanding" (Philippians 4:7), and "the love of Christ that surpasses knowledge" (Ephesians 3:19) will someday be my eternal inheritance.

When faith clings to these as its present possession, the fruit is tangible spiritual joy. How to live in the presence of that joy is the subject of this little book.

One
SPEAKING THE LANGUAGE OF HUMILITY

Jeff's alarm rattles him awake on a cold winter morning. He groans, sits up, and maneuvers his feet onto the chilly floor. With great sincerity he bows his head and mumbles a prayer under his breath, "Father, thank you for a good night's sleep. Thank you for the soft mattress and warm blankets. God, I am even thankful for the alarm clock."

He stumbles to the bathroom, eyelids half shut, mind partially in gear, and reaches for the electric razor. "Father, thank you for this shaver. Most people throughout history have shaved with a knife, if at all. And while I am at it, thank you for heating and lights."

He gropes his way to the kitchen and switches on the coffee pot. "Father, thank you for this wonderful device—a gift from you. I am so grateful. Hot, fresh coffee in two minutes! What a privilege. God, you are so good to me."

Returning to his bedroom, he opens his closet to find it full of shirts, slacks, and shoes. Just the day before he had read that the average father in Southeast Asia feeds his family on $100 per month with nothing left for clothing. So Jeff prays, "Father, how great is your grace. Thank you for these material blessings. I am so unworthy."

He dresses and settles into his favorite chair for prayer and Bible reading. Now he comes to the real reason for gratitude. "Father, thank you for the gospel. You chose me from before the foundation of the world to be holy and blameless in your sight. Why me? It wasn't my virtues. You didn't foresee goodness in me. That is clear. It was astounding love and grace given without assignable cause, plain and simple. Father, thank you for sending your Son to rescue me from the futile ways of my forefathers. Thank you for saving me from the wrath to come. Thank you for saving me from hell. You sent your Son to experience the painful wrath I deserve. You did this to unite us in friendship and love. How can I comprehend such mercy? How can I thank you enough? I am so grateful for your kindness. Thank you for showing amazing grace to an unworthy sinner."

Because Jeff knows what he deserves, he takes nothing for granted.

"And Father, while I'm at it, thank you for this Bible. Most Christians have never owned one, nor would they have been able to read one if they had, but

I have six different translations and could easily buy more. I am so grateful."

And also, "Thank you for my wife and three children. Yes, there are problems. It is not all roses. None of us in this family is perfect. Sometimes there is conflict, but I want to thank you for your obvious grace in all our lives."

On the way to work he inventories his schedule. At 10:00 he must mediate a conflict between two subordinates. "Father, thank you for this problem. How good of you to allow me to help these two men. I don't know how I am going to resolve this conflict, but I want to thank you in advance for the grace that you will provide."

Lunch arrives. He bows his head in deep and profound gratitude. He knows that 85 percent of the world lives on less than $200 per month and that huge swaths of the world's population go to bed hungry every night. He deserves worse, and he knows it. He doesn't say grace perfunctorily or mechanically. He prays a short prayer of profound, heart-felt gratitude.

Can you relate to Jeff? Probably not. He sounds a bit Pollyanna, maybe even over-the-top. If you are like most Christians, you know you need to be more thankful, but for you gratitude is a fly-over virtue. Yes, you are grateful in a general, low-level way. Perhaps you say grace at every meal, but your thanksgiving is often mechanical, not especially sincere. And if you're honest, many times it doesn't even cross your mind to give thanks to

God. You know you are supposed to be grateful, but you rarely think about it. Most significantly, you don't consider this a big deal. Instead of giving thanks in all circumstances, you often grumble, complain, and give in to self-pity. But come on, doesn't everyone? What's the big deal? Doesn't God know we are human?

Goodness, Glory, and Gratitude

I understand that perspective. Yes, God knows we are frail. He knows we have a rebellious sin nature. But in this book I want you to see the bigger picture. I want you to see that the absence of gratitude can only mean one thing—the presence of self-pity as well as the grumbling and complaining that are its fruits.

The truth is that grumbling, complaining, and self-pity are rampant and violent statements of unbelief. They are the opposite of godward gratitude. They reject the gospel. They reject the reality of my sinfulness. They say, "I deserve only good things from God." They deny my absolute dependence *on* God. They deny his sovereignty and his goodness—essential aspects of his deity. And they are guaranteed to leave me a far weaker, far less effective, and far less joyful Christian.

God certainly understands that we are "only human." But what he wants *for* us and *from* us is a joyful and humble heart. And a heart like that can only come from gratitude. Gratitude is foundational to vibrant, healthy Christianity.

God created us for his glory, and a synonym for

God's glory is his goodness (Exodus 33:18–19). A heart that overflows with thanksgiving, despite troubling and challenging circumstances, is a heart confident in that goodness. It displays that confidence through gratitude. Gratitude therefore magnifies God's goodness—it magnifies his glory.

The failure to overflow with gratitude in the face of trouble reveals a loss of confidence in God's goodness. A heart captured by grumbling, complaining, and self-pity says, "I deserve better than I am getting, and God is not *good enough* to give it to me." This is an attack on God's glory, and it sends a clear message: God isn't good. He cannot be trusted.

God values nothing more than magnifying and displaying his glory. This is why throughout redemptive history he has responded decisively to grumbling and complaining among his people. When God judged Korah, Dathan, and Abiram the Israelites grumbled, and in response God put 14,700 of them to death (Numbers 16:49). Indeed, it was the rebellion of ingratitude that kept the Israelites wandering in the wilderness until an entire generation had passed away. God even said that their complaining was an act of *despising* him (Numbers 14:11). I'm sure that when you and I are ungrateful we have not decided to despise God, yet that is exactly how God sees it, for in truth that is what we are doing.

Paul knew all this, and he was committed to living for the glory of God, so he consistently emphasized gratitude in his letters. In fact, he exulted in it. "In *everything* by prayer and supplication *with thanksgiving* let your requests be made known to God" (Philippians 4:6).

He also sought to *practice* gratitude in all circumstances. The Corinthian church tolerated members who practiced incest, got drunk at communion, and even denied the resurrection, yet Paul began his letter to them by expressing gratitude for them. "I give thanks to my God always for you because of the grace of God that was given you in Christ Jesus" (1 Corinthians 1:4).

This was not flattery. Paul was sincere. Notice how he exhorted the early Christians to relate to each other: "Let there be no filthiness nor foolish talk nor crude joking, which are out of place, but instead *let there be thanksgiving*" (Ephesians 5:4). Writing to the church at Colossae his language was even stronger: "So walk in him…*abounding* in thanksgiving" (Colossians 2:6–7). Some translate abounding as "overflowing," like a bucket already filled to the brim, with still more water pouring into it, drenching the ground beneath.

How about corporate worship? Paul's exhortation here hits the exact same note: "Singing and making melody to the Lord with all your heart, *giving thanks always and for everything* to God the Father in the name of our Lord Jesus Christ" (Ephesians 5:19–20).

In fact, we can sum up Paul's exhortations this way: gratitude to God is the Christian's right and proper response every time. No exceptions. "Give thanks *in all circumstances*; for this is the will of God in Christ Jesus for you" (1 Thessalonians 5:18).

We should pray with thanksgiving. We should worship with thanksgiving. We should speak with thanksgiving. We should react to every circumstance in life with thanksgiving. We should constantly think and act from an active disposition and intention to be thankful. The glory of God is at stake.

So let's return to our friend, Jeff. Was his gratitude excessive? In light of these texts, I don't think so. Based on Paul's exhortations, Jeff was just trying to practice biblical Christianity. He was merely responding with appropriate gratitude to what the Bible teaches us about God, man, creation, and redemption. What might seem excessive to us was merely a fervent attempt to be biblical, to be godly, to be what the Bible urges us all to be. Gratitude and thanksgiving are not fly-over virtues. Just the opposite. They are at the very heart of true Christian virtue and essential to godliness. Do you and I see it this way?

I'm not suggesting that the only right way to respond to Paul's exhortations is to walk through your day continually verbalizing your gratitude in a nonstop stream of consciousness. But I am saying that the *heart attitude* we see in Jeff's example is far from excessive and probably a lot closer to God's desire for us than most of us live on a daily basis.

How do we become more like Jeff, more like the kind of Christian Paul exhorts us to be? How do we become people who are genuinely grateful to God—in the mountain-top experiences when everything is great, in the mundane moments of daily life, and even in deep trials?

First, let's make sure we have a basic understanding of gratitude from a biblical perspective.

Grasping Gratitude

The social sciences confirm what is fairly obvious to begin with: gratitude doesn't come naturally. Children must be trained to show it. Gratitude to others is part of being polite or having good manners; but you can be a model of etiquette and never get anywhere near the biblical idea of gratitude. In her book, *The Gift of Thanks,* Margaret Visser observes that "polite people" may say "thank you" up to 100 times per day and yet experience "little or no grateful emotion."[1] That is, they go through the motions of politeness but without heartfelt gratitude. In fact, outward expressions of politeness can easily emerge from mixed motives. Consider the teenage girl who thanks her father sweetly for the loan of his car—mostly in the hope that he will let her borrow it again.

Biblical gratitude, however, is so much more than social conventions. Paul's exhortations to be thankful do not proceed from a concern for etiquette and politeness—however sincere or well-intentioned—but from a passion to glorify God. This is because true thanksgiving is not an external formality, a matter of words or gestures or tone of voice. It is a natural outpouring of an awareness of three things:

1. our creaturehood,
2. what we rightly deserve before God's holiness, and
3. the gracious redemption God has given to us through his Son.

Creaturehood. God created me. If he hadn't, I wouldn't exist. As Paul put it, "The God who made the world and everything in it, being Lord of heaven and earth…gives to all mankind life and breath and *everything*" (Acts 17:24–25). Everything I am and possess is God's gift.

This means that all the essential elements that make us who we are were given to us by God. Our talents, intelligence, height, appearance, parents, country of birth, the generation we were born into — we decided none of it. Yet these are the kind of factors that determine so much of our life's outcome. All of these, and infinitely more, are God's gifts. They were *given to us creatures by a gracious Creator.* For this reason, the object of true gratitude is always ultimately God.

What we deserve. Our natural tendency is to take credit for our gifts. The blustering business tycoon, the self-glorifying athlete, and the preening pop star are just exaggerated versions of the rest of us in this regard. We all want to boast and brag and be seen as special.

But as creatures, boasting is the speech of naked arrogance. It actually implies a claim to deity, as if we created ourselves and decided what gifts and talents we would possess. It is the opposite of gratitude and just one of countless manifestations of the sin nature we have all inherited from Adam. In his infinite holiness, God finds this sin nature, and each one of our specific acts of sin, infinitely repulsive. As a result, all we truly deserve from God is judgment for our rebellious, ungrateful hearts.

The gift of redemption. Despite the judgment we deserve, in his grace God has redeemed us and given us eternal life. This gift has a value beyond all measure, and was purchased at infinite cost, a subject we will return to later in this book. It is a gift that deserves constant gratitude.

The Greek word *eucharisteo* encapsulates the essential connection between gratitude and grace. We usually translate it into our English word *thanks* or *thanksgiving*. But notice that the word *charis*—Greek for "gift" or "grace"—is right there in the middle of the word. This grace is unmerited favor, favor given to those who deserve only punishment. Gratitude for the grace of God is therefore literally central to biblical thanksgiving.

This is the perspective of my friend, Curtis. Whenever I ask how he is doing, he responds, "Better than I deserve." His speech expresses a heart constantly aware of the cross. Here is what he is thinking. "I *deserve crucifixion,* and I am not getting it. In fact, I will never get it, and the reason is God's amazing grace and love. I will never get the judgment I deserve. Christ went to the cross and took the judgment that I deserve in my place. That is why, for eternity, I will never cease to abound with thanksgiving. Jesus took the judgment I deserve so that I could receive the reward he deserves."

Until we understand what we truly deserve from God, grace has no meaning, and we will have little real motivation for gratitude. The well-spring of all Christian thanksgiving is a clear understanding of the redemption given to us through the cross.

To summarize, biblical gratitude is rooted in the recognition that I have been given undeserved gifts, both natural and spiritual. Thankfulness expresses my creatureliness and God's sovereignty. It reflects awareness of and gladness in the fact that God is God, and I am not. Biblical gratitude is always anchored in this sense of dependence on God. It is the language of those who know they are creatures, and it is the proper response to redemption.

This is why thanksgiving is the language of humility—because true gratitude arises from a realization of our weakness and need. People with grateful hearts live with an awareness of just how much God has done for them.

An Old Testament Picture

There is a vivid picture of this reality in Psalm 50. Gratitude was the response that God sought from the

Old Testament sacrificial system. The Psalm opens with a description of the Day of Judgment. "Our God comes…before him is a devouring fire, around him a mighty tempest. He calls to the heavens above and to the earth, that he may judge his people" (vv 3–4).

Next God describes the sacrificial system. We are reminded that God the Creator owns everything. Ultimately, he doesn't want or need the animals that the Jews offer in sacrifice.

Then the psalmist tells us what God really wants— *the sacrifice of thanksgiving*. "Offer to God a sacrifice of thanksgiving, and perform your vows to the Most High" (v 14). This is a vital point we must not miss: *thanksgiving sums up all that God sought from the sacrificial system*. We can easily get distracted by the outward aspects of the sacrificial system—the rules and rituals, the blood and death. But the point of it all was that the Israelites would live with continual, dramatic reminders that they were completely dependent upon God and therefore ought to be endlessly grateful.

This was especially obvious in the sin offering. First, the worshiper laid his hand on the animal to be sacrificed. This symbolized the transfer of his guilt to the animal. The beast was then slaughtered in the worshiper's *presence* and in the worshiper's *place*. The message embedded in this ritual was clear:

- The worshiper is a sinner.
- The penalty for sin is death.

- The worshiper therefore deserves to die.
- But God offers a substitute sacrifice to die in the worshiper's place.

The Old Testament sacrificial system was therefore all about substitution. It was designed to be a picture of grace, producing humility (the fruit of grace) and thanksgiving (the right response to grace). But as Israel routinely repeated the sacrifices generation after generation, they lost sight of the true meaning. They forgot that humility, expressing itself through thanksgiving, was the fruit God wanted. In fact, in verses 12–13 we see that the Israelites had actually begun to think God was hungry and wanted meat! God inspired Psalm 50 to remind Israel that thanksgiving, not the animal, was the point.

So there was really just one thing God wanted from the Old Testament worshiper: gratitude. Deep, heartfelt, overflowing gratitude to a gracious and merciful God. A God who allowed a substitute to die in his place. A God who forgives his enemies—you and me—at the substitute's expense.

A New Testament Reality

The book of Hebrews summarizes the matter with an exhortation. Speaking of Jesus and his substitutionary sacrifice on the cross for us, it says, "Through him then let us continually offer up a sacrifice of praise to God, that is, the fruit of lips that acknowledge his name" (Hebrews 13:15).

The true sacrifice God seeks *was* and *still is* gratitude, rooted in humility. How much more should we overflow with thanksgiving now that the ultimate sacrifice has come to bear God's wrath? On the day of final judgment God will come looking for the fruit of thanksgiving from humble lips. A life given to joyful gratitude testifies that we understand the gospel—we have internalized the grace that flows from the ultimate sacrifice given to us through the gospel.

God makes amazing promises to those who cultivate a humble heart of gratitude. For example:

- God exalts the humble (James 4:10).
- He dwells with the lowly (Isaiah 57:15).
- He exalts those who humble themselves (Philippians 2:5–11).
- He lifts up the humble (Psalm 147:6).
- He gives grace to the humble (James 4:6).
- He looks favorably to the humble (Isaiah 66:2).
- He honors the humble (Proverbs 15:33).

Biblical thanksgiving always proceeds from a humble heart. It does not act *in order* to get something from God, but it *will* attract God's lavish, gracious attention. Not surprisingly, God takes the opposite attitude toward those who display the opposite of humility.

- He humbles the proud (Ezekiel 17:24).

- He opposes the proud (James 4:6).
- He withdraws from the proud (Psalm 138:6).
- He promises to bring down the proud (Proverbs 18:12; 29:23).

If I really believe God's promise to bless the humble and judge the proud, I will pursue humility.

And what is the language of humility? Thanksgiving. Expressions of thanksgiving to God and others are signs of the humility that God delights to bless. Jesus said, "Out of the abundance of the heart his mouth speaks" (Luke 6:45). A humble heart will increasingly express gratitude.

Paul saw that the failure to be thankful to God is at the very heart of sinfulness. Trying to get to the bottom of the basic sin of his day (and ours) he wrote, "Although they knew God, they did not honor him as God or *give thanks to him*, but they became futile in their thinking, and their foolish hearts were darkened" (Romans 1:21).

Paul then shows how sinful practices are rooted in the refusal to give God thanks. Commenting on the passage, *Eerdman's Bible Dictionary* notes, "The fundamental sin of the Gentiles is said to be their failure to 'honor him as God or give thanks to him' (Romans 1:21)."[2]

Nothing has changed today. Paul was referring to unbelievers, but the same is true for Christians. Pride is still the great sin leading to all others, and lack of gratitude is still a clear sign of a proud heart.

Because we are proud, we are not grateful. And we are proud because we do not really believe the gospel.

Where We Go from Here

If the story of Jeff that opened this chapter seems too good to be true, maybe we should give thanksgiving another look. Is it possible to be grateful enough? What does it look like to be someone who abounds with thanksgiving?

Thankful people are happy people. In his commentary on Matthew, Michael Green recounts the story of a fourteenth-century German mystic named Johann Tauler. One day Tauler met a beggar.

> "God give you a good day, my friend," he said.
>
> The beggar answered, "I thank God I never had a bad one."
>
> Then Tauler said, "God give you a happy life, my friend."
>
> "I thank God," said the beggar, "that I am never unhappy."
>
> In amazement Tauler asked, "What do you mean?"
>
> "Well," said the beggar, "when it is fine I thank God. When it rains I thank God. When I have plenty I thank God. When I am hungry I thank God. And, since God's will is my will, and whatever pleases him pleases me, why should I say I am unhappy when I am not?"

Tauler looked at the man in astonishment. "Who are you?" he asked.

"I am a king," said the beggar.

"Where, then, is your kingdom?" asked Tauler.

The beggar replied quietly, "In my heart."[3]

The secret to the beggar's happiness was his gratitude. Grateful people are happy people. Gratitude is the secret of spiritual joy!

Therefore, let us cultivate the discipline of gratitude. To do this we must flee the opposite—complaining, grumbling, self-pity, boasting, and the like. In future chapters we will examine these sins, but first we need to take a hard look at another reason for gratitude. This chapter has posited the cross as the ground of our gratitude. But we should also overflow with thanksgiving because God is both sovereign and good.

Two

CELEBRATING A SOVEREIGN AND GOOD GOD

A heart overflowing with gratitude matters greatly, but should Christians be grateful at all times? How about times of unusual stress or suffering? Does God expect a person experiencing clinical depression to be grateful? How about a mother who just found out that her 4-year-old has brain cancer? Should someone being tortured for the gospel be grateful? Should a husband whose wife is having an affair be grateful?

The biblical answer is yes, and the reason is simple: God is absolutely sovereign, and God is infinitely good. The cross of Christ is the greatest illustration of this principle in history.

Bad Things Happen

A well-known book by Rabbi Harold Kushner wrestles with an issue that philosophers have been pondering for ages: the question of evil. Essentially, the book asks: if God is good, why does he allow bad things to happen to good people?

From a Christian perspective, this is actually the wrong question. The Bible is perfectly clear that all people are sinners. In fact, "no one does good" (Romans 3:12). In God's eyes, although some people certainly are less sinful than others, none of us are actually *good*. None of us can stand before a holy God.

We are all "bad people" who deserve to have "bad things" happen to us. Indeed, we deserve nothing less than God's full wrath, both now and in the future. What amazes biblically informed Christians, therefore, is not trouble. What amazes them is that every day God expresses his goodness to billions who deserve nothing but judgment. He continues to give sinful rebels like you and me food and air and water—life and breath and everything else—day after day, century after century.

This is not to say, however, that examining Rabbi Kushner's question can't be helpful for believers. Even though the wrath of God has been removed from us, we still suffer, sometimes incredibly. Believers in Jesus have been loved by God from before the foundation of the world (Ephesians 1:4). As Jesus put it, "As the Father has loved me, so have I loved you. Abide in my love" (John 15:9). So for us, there is a question that's definitely worth asking: if God is good and God is sovereign, why would he allow those he loves to suffer?

William Tyndale (1494–1536) is a good example. He was one of the early English Reformers and the first person to translate the Greek New Testament into English. This work made him an enemy of the English government. In fact, King Henry VIII commanded his secret police to hunt Tyndale down and kill him, so Tyndale fled to continental Europe and went into hiding. After finishing his New Testament, Tyndale smuggled copies back into England. Despite the fact that the penalty for merely owning one was death, many English families secretly acquired them. Such was the hunger for God's word and the need for Tyndale's courageous mission.

Next, Tyndale applied himself to translating the Old Testament from the original Hebrew. Working from sunup to sundown, without central heat or air conditioning, lonely, and in fear of King Henry's secret police, he modeled love, self-denial, and perseverance. He began with the Pentateuch—the first five books of the Old Testament. After months of arduous, taxing labor, he completed the task. Then in 1529 he boarded a ship to sail from Holland to Hamburg, but a storm wrecked the vessel. Tyndale's original Pentateuch translation went overboard. He had no other copies; all his work was gone. His biographer, Brian Edwards, writes, "Tyndale lost his money, valuable time, and the fruit of months of hard labor…How Tyndale felt as he boarded another vessel and arrived in Hamburg is not hard to imagine."[4]

It took another nine months of intense, mind-numbing labor to replicate his work. Why would God allow circumstances like this to happen to one of his children?

Skip forward two hundred years to William Carey (1761–1834), the founder of the modern missionary movement. Like Tyndale, Carey was a linguistic genius who used his talents to translate the Bible. His field of operation was India, a subcontinent with hundreds of languages and even more dialects. In 1812 his warehouse caught fire. It contained thousands of hours of translating work. It also included his printing presses and many rare fonts used to print in obscure languages. "Carey was the chief sufferer," notes his biographer. "Lost were nearly all his Indian Scripture versions; all his Kanarese New Testament; two whole, large Old Testament books in Sanskrit; many pages of his *Bengali Dictionary;* all his *Telugu Grammar,* etc."[5]

This was a major blow, one that would have derailed a lesser man. But Carey was used to trial. His first wife had died of mental illness. Nevertheless, Carey was devastated. "In one night," he wrote to a friend, "the labors of years are consumed. How unsearchable are the divine ways!"[6]

Troubles, trials, stresses, losses, and persecutions come to the best of God's children. A 9-year-old falls off the monkey bars, breaks his neck, and dies. A father and successful businessman sustains a brain injury that renders him a vegetable, and he lives on in that condition for twenty years. The real estate market collapses, and a wealthy retiree loses everything, forced to start over like a 25-year-old.

When troubles like these happen, how does God want his people to respond?

The Test of Faith

How great thinkers respond to suffering and tragedy can alter the destiny of nations. The Enlightenment, the eighteenth century intellectual movement that has done much damage to the Christian faith and the modern world, was partially caused by a wrong response to suffering. The Lisbon Earthquake of 1755 provoked three architects of the Enlightenment (and therefore of the modern world)—Voltaire (1694–1778), Rousseau (1712–1778), and Kant (1724–1804)—to reject the idea that God is both good and sovereign.

Humanly speaking, this was understandable. The earthquake was a catastrophe. Geologists estimate that it was a 9 on the 10-point Richter scale and killed some 40,000 to 60,000 people, which would make it one of the deadliest earthquakes in history.[7] A tsunami and fires quickly followed the earthquake, almost totally destroying the city.

Such extreme suffering prompted Voltaire, Rousseau, and Kant to reject the idea that God is both sovereign and good. If he were both, they reasoned, he would never have allowed this to happen—therefore he is either good but not in control, or he is in control but not good. This thinking popularized a kind of Deism, the belief that God exists but has little ongoing involvement in human affairs and very little in common with the God of the Bible.

Today, the western world is still heavily influenced by Deism in various forms, infecting even the thinking of a great many Christians. It can alter how people respond to suffering and catastrophe on the individual level and the social level. Therefore it can change, not only the destiny of nations, but the long-term trajectory of our personal lives.

Elizabeth's life has been difficult. Diagnosed with breast cancer at age twenty, she went through a painful bout of chemotherapy and recovered. Five years later the doctors discovered more cancer, this time in her uterus. Again, more chemotherapy. Today she is in her thirties. She attends church and believes the gospel, but her response to these tragic circumstances has shriveled her relationship with God. She is a spiritual pigmy marked by bitterness, pessimism, and fear. She has a difficult time trusting God for the present or her future, and is often not pleasant to be around.

Jack is an interesting comparison. At age 41 he lost his wife of twenty years to cancer. Three years later his oldest daughter was killed in a head-on car accident. In contrast to Elizabeth, Jack walked through the terrible pain of these twin losses by habitually offering God the sacrifice of thanksgiving. This habit was costly. Jack did not feel grateful, but by faith he thanked God anyway.

Despite struggling with depression and despair, he clung to the truth that God is both sovereign and good. He believed that God would use his sorrow for good. This was five years ago. Today Jack is a robust, joyful, hope-filled believer. He excels in compassion and perseverance. There is no one I would rather be around. He encourages everyone he meets.

My brother, Bruce, brought me to Christ. He was a lot like Jack, a model of gratitude in adversity. At age 56, Bruce was diagnosed with glioblastoma, an aggressive form of brain cancer. Ninety percent die within two years. When the nurse came to wheel him into his first surgery, Bruce was reading A.W. Pink's *The Sovereignty of God.* My brother was a man of faith. He believed that God is both good and sovereign, and he rejoiced with simple child-like trust.

Bruce died two years later, but he left this world glorifying God with thanksgiving. Here is an entry from my diary during the year between his diagnosis and his death.

> *Bruce and I celebrated his 57th birthday. It might be our last birthday lunch together. (It was.) We talked very frankly and openly about his impending death. He is pessimistic about recovery. His face was swollen from steroids, speech slow, and memory bad, moving like an old, old man. He related a bout of disorientation that occurred last week. Didn't know where he was again. Another time he got so ill while*

driving that he had to pull off the road and sit down on a bench for two hours. Didn't know the cause. He is having difficulty recognizing faces, and his hearing has been permanently damaged by radiation.

In the midst of this suffering, however, my brother constantly thanked God. "This last year has given me time to get my estate and life in order," he said. He repeatedly thanked God for how good his life had been. He thanked God for his salvation, for his cancer, and for how God was using the pain and trauma to shape his character. Until the disease stole his ability to think clearly, he continued to glorify God with thanksgiving.

This is what it looks like when trouble comes to one who really believes. When times are incredibly hard and we have no idea why, gratitude says to God, "I don't understand this pain. I don't know why you have allowed this, but I trust you. You are good, and you are sovereign. I trust that you love me and that you have orchestrated these circumstances for my good. My life is in your hands, and there is no place I would rather be."

Suffering exposes what we *really* believe, not what we say we believe. Some, like Bruce and Jack, respond with faith. They seek God, deepen their relationships with him, and their troubles enhance their fruitfulness. Others, like Rousseau, Voltaire, Kant, and Elizabeth respond either by blaming God, lapsing into self-pity, or grumbling. Any spiritual fruit that survives is emaciated and shriveled.

The deciding factor between fruitful and unfruitful suffering is the presence or absence of faith. Do we really believe God is both sovereign and good, and on that basis offer the sacrifice of thanksgiving? Or do we complain, pout, indulge in self-pity, and withdraw into similar expressions of unbelief?

The real world is fallen. Because we live in it, our responses are also often fallen. I recently went through a time of severe stress. In my head I knew God was at work, but he seemed a million miles away. At times I became despondent. I forgot to thank him. And when the thought crossed my mind, the effort to respond obediently took all my energy. At times like this the cross of Christ is our refuge. "God, you know my weakness. Have mercy on my sinful soul. You bore the wrath that my ungrateful heart deserves. Lord, I am grateful for one fact: Christ's heart of gratitude has been freely imputed to my sinful self." (We'll learn more about this amazing truth in chapter three.)

Because the Bible testifies to God's comprehensive sovereignty and goodness, we can respond to life's troubles with gratitude. Is this how you typically react to trouble, persecution, rejection, problems, depression, sins against you, and the pain of your own sin?

God is Sovereign

We have learned that our response to adversity can impact nations and powerfully shape our personal character. We have also learned that confidence in the sovereignty of God, rightly understood, is the first ground of a grateful heart.

In his book, *The Doctrine of God,* John Frame notes that of all God's attributes, sovereignty is the most frequently referenced in Scripture.[8] For example, "Whatever the LORD pleases, he does" (Psalm 135:6). God's sovereignty is also exhaustive. Not one sparrow falls from the bush, not one hair from your head, without God's permission (Matthew 10:29–30).

When I discovered that my 4-year-old grandson had a brain tumor, this glorious truth sustained me. The sovereignty of God has also fortified me to face the future. When I heard that a friend had cancer, I didn't respond by dreading the future, thinking the same could happen to me. Why? Every detail of my future is in God's hands, and he loves me with an infinite love. I am not saying I won't suffer. I am saying that should I suffer, God will use it for his glory and my eternal happiness. Ultimately, it will be a blessing. The sovereignty of God is such a glorious truth! It is an anchor for the believer's soul.

God's sovereignty is so exhaustive that he even uses our sins for good. For example, God orchestrated Samson's sinful marriage to an unbelieving Philistine to bring about good. Samson's "father and mother did not know that [Samson's marriage] was from the LORD, for [God] was seeking an opportunity against the Philistines" (Judges 14:4).

God also uses sins committed against us for our

good. Think of Joseph. His brothers sinned against him, selling him into slavery. But years later, God used that sin against Joseph to make him prime minister of Egypt. When Joseph revealed himself to his brothers, he said, "Do not be distressed or angry with yourselves because you sold me here, for *God sent me before you* to preserve life" (Genesis 45:5).

God also orchestrates and uses social disasters for our good and his glory. Amos 3:6 is God's answer to the Lisbon earthquake. "Does disaster come to a city, unless the LORD has done it?"

This is why, at the end of a long dissertation on God's plan for the Jews (Romans 9–11), Paul sums up the passage with these words. "For from him and through him and to him are *all things*. To him be glory forever" (Romans 11:36). What are the "all things" Paul has in mind? First, God's judicial hardening of the Jewish people so that they cannot hear and respond to the gospel. Second, God's election of some to salvation and rejection of others. And last, the whole contorted history of the Jewish people. "All things" good and evil are under God's complete control. He is absolutely sovereign. "Confidence in the sovereignty of God in all that affects us," notes Jerry Bridges, "is crucial to our trusting him. If there is a single event in all of the universe that can occur outside of God's sovereign control, then we cannot trust him."[9]

In addition, God is sovereign over the human heart, over the rise and fall of civilizations, over the evil deeds of nations, over the good and evil that we do, over our sanity, over the sins of others towards us, and even over our own sins.

We must also note that while God is utterly sovereign, this never eliminates, denies, or frustrates human responsibility. God never tempts people to sin (James 1:13). Each individual is completely responsible for his own sin. We are not robots. We make real decisions, and for each of them we will someday give an account. The Bible is clear that there is a sense in which God allows, and even brings sin to pass, for his glory. How these two ideas—God's sovereignty and human responsibility—go together perfectly is a mystery, and faithful Christians are willing to let it remain imperfectly resolved.

One thing this all means is that no evil can touch you—whether the betrayal of a friend, your personal sin, the death of a loved one, the collapse of the stock market, or the unraveling of a nation-state—without God's express permission. As we mentioned earlier, this would be a problem if God were not good. But the one who is sovereign is also infinitely good, and that brings us to our second principle for this chapter.

God is Good

Today, most people who believe God exists take his goodness for granted. But it has not always been this way. Neither Moses nor Israel really understood God's essential goodness. That is why Moses asked to see

God's glory. He wanted to see into the heart of God's basic nature. Imagine Moses' astonishment when God responded with these amazing words. "The LORD, the LORD, a God merciful and gracious, slow to anger, and abounding in steadfast love and faithfulness, keeping steadfast love for thousands, forgiving iniquity and transgression and sin" (Exodus 34:6–7). From this point forward the Bible gives these two verses prominence. All or part of them are repeated multiple times in the Old Testament.[10]

God is not fickle, and he does not change. He never quits being good. He is always *for* his saints. He is always on our side. "If God is *for* us, who can be against us?" (Romans 8:31). To confirm the truth of these words God eventually sent his Son to the cross. There we see a graphic picture of his essential nature, his glory, as originally revealed to Moses.

God is an everlasting Father who loves his children with an everlasting love. Like a good father, he allows pain, but it is always an expression of his paternal discipline. It does not express his wrath or condemnation. He shapes and forms us with his discipline so that we can share more of his holiness.

> *For the Lord disciplines the one he loves*, and chastises every son whom he receives…God is treating you as sons. For what son is there whom his father does not discipline? If you are left without discipline, in which all have participated,

then you are illegitimate children and not sons…
he disciplines us for our good, that we may share
his holiness. For the moment all discipline seems
painful rather than pleasant, but later it yields the
peaceful fruit of righteousness to those who have
been trained by it (Hebrews 12:6–11).

Holiness is God's aim, and holiness and happiness
go together. *Holy people are happy people!*

God's discipline is comprehensive. As we have seen,
he even uses our sins and the sins committed against us
for our ultimate welfare. He uses them to humble us.
He uses them to deepen our dependence upon him. He
uses them to communicate the vastness of his personal
love for needy, unworthy sinners.

Think of Peter. God used Peter's betrayal of Jesus
to humble him, to transfer his trust from self to God.
The humbling that Peter's sin produced equipped him
for his ultimate earthly role: apostle to the Jews.

Sovereignty and Goodness at the Cross

Many believers struggle to fully accept the sovereignty
and goodness of God. How do they go together?
Could something this wonderful really be true? Is it
really biblical? The answer is not found on the fringes.
It is found at the center of the biblical story: the cross
of Christ. The cross is the most potent fusion of God's
sovereignty and God's goodness in history.

The cross is a dramatic demonstration of God's sovereignty. God planned every moment of his Son's execution. We know this because God predicted it in detail centuries in advance.[11] Without tempting or causing anyone to sin, God brought each of those details to pass. The Jewish people betrayed Jesus. In callous cruelty, Pontius Pilate gave him over to crucifixion. Although God did not incite Pilate to evil, God controlled everything Pilate did. He left nothing to chance. Without violating the moral responsibility of the Jews or Romans, God's hand controlled every detail.

The pain that came to the man God loved the most, his Son, was excruciating. Jesus went before us as the model man. Therefore, because God is good, he used the pain of the cross to shape him. He was made perfect through suffering (Hebrews 2:10). "He learned obedience through what he suffered" (Hebrews 5:8). In fact, God is so good that he even used the cross to save many of those who conspired to kill his Son. That's right. *God is so good* that he used the sinful rejection of the Jews to turn around and save the very people who crucified him in spiteful malice.

Peter's speech in Acts 2 makes all of this clear. "This Jesus, delivered up according to the *definite plan and foreknowledge of God*, you crucified and killed by the hands of lawless men" (Acts 2:23). Peter wants us to know that the cosmic crime of Messiah-murder was a "definite plan" that God "fulfilled." Here is the most amazing display of goodness in history! God used the sins of his enemies to reconcile some of those very same enemies to himself. Truly God is sovereign, and truly God is *infinitely* good. What can we say? Our mouths are stopped in wonder. The cross is the clearest statement of these facts in human history.

In Everything

With all of this in mind Paul penned Romans 8:28, "And we know that for those who love God all things work together for good, for those who are called according to his purpose." Paul was convinced that every circumstance in life is part of God's plan to ultimately maximize his blessing to his children. We do not always see *how* God has designed our sufferings to enhance our joy, but if we understand the Bible's teaching on this subject, we trust that God is bringing about this wonderful result. We believe this because a good God works in and through all things, and therefore controls all things.

If all this is true, how should we respond? God wants us to overflow with thanksgiving—and that is exactly how the apostle Paul exhorts us to live. God wants us to be grateful in good times and bad times. Paul wants us to give thanks for the way God is using the sins of others against us. He wants us to thank God for the way he will use our own sins for good. Yes, God might discipline us, and it might be painful, but God is a Father who loves us. As he did with his Son, he will use our pain for our good. We can thank God for the difficult circumstances he has orchestrated.

For these reasons Paul makes many expansive, all-inclusive exhortations to live in constant gratitude. We noted most of them in the previous chapter. For example, "Give thanks in *all circumstances*; for this is the will of God in Christ Jesus for you" (1 Thessalonians 5:18).

Paul also wants us to mingle our intercession with thanksgiving. "Do not be anxious about anything, but in everything by prayer and supplication *with thanksgiving* let your requests be made known to God" (Philippians 4:6). Our lives are, in the apostle Paul's words, to "abound" or overflow "with thanksgiving" (Colossians 2:7).

In summary, we have explored two grounds for a life of gratitude. In chapter one we learned that we are always doing better than we deserve. In this chapter we learned that God is both sovereign and good. The cross is the graphic display of both principles. All of life's circumstances are in God's hands, and he means us good not evil.

The next two chapters will pause to examine two enemies of thanksgiving: grumbling and self-pity.

Three
GETTING A GRIP ON GRUMBLING

We saw in chapter one that thanksgiving flows from a grateful heart. It is the language of humility. Grumbling and complaining are the vernacular of the proud. You cannot be thankful and complain at the same time. These attitudes are mutually exclusive.

However, if you are like me, thanksgiving does not always describe you. Sometimes you give in to grumbling and complaining. You do not obey Paul's exhortation to "Do all things without grumbling or questioning" (Philippians 2:14).

I was in business for many years. I had to manage my time carefully. I prioritized each day's events, watched over a tight calendar, and was careful not to give in to the tyranny of the urgent. These skills enabled me to simultaneously run a business, parent my children, be a husband to my wife, and serve as an elder in my church.

Eventually, however, time management became too important to me. In biblical terms it became an idol.

When I transitioned into full-time ministry, God began to deal with it, and my computer was the tool he used.

I spend most of my day on my computer. I do my Bible study there. My prayer lists are there. In addition, my computer contains my calendar, my contact lists, and my all-too-crucial "to do" list. The computer is where I prepare sermons, handle email, and write articles and books. It is the functional hub around which my life revolves.

Many people have never had a hard drive crash, but in the last ten years it has happened to me four times. You read that right—*four times!* A fifth time I had to format my hard drive—a similar procedure, although not quite as complicated.

Each crash has flushed several days from my schedule. Even with my data backed up elsewhere, it has taken several days to format the new hard drive, replace my programs, settings, and so forth. In other words, for someone to whom efficiency matters, a hard drive crash is the worst of all possible scenarios.

The last time this happened the timing was especially difficult. My Sunday sermon was due. A manuscript had arrived from my publisher that needed editing by a deadline. Meetings and the assorted people-problems that fill up a pastor's week dotted my calendar. *Not again,* I thought. *I can't believe this is happening to me now? I don't have time for this.*

I simmered. I fussed. I fumed. In short, I grumbled and complained.

My head knew that "for those who love God all things work together for good" (Romans 8:28), but I was not feeling it. Instead, I was a volcano of frustration on the edge of eruption. Deep down inside I was throwing what Southerners call a "hissy fit."

God spoke to Balaam through a donkey. In my case he used someone more attractive and smarter. "If your congregation could only see you now," my lovely wife observed. "The one always exhorting them to be thankful—because God is so good—isn't very thankful today, is he?"

She was right. I was wearing my heart on my sleeve. I was not happy with how God had sovereignly chosen to distribute my time. My actions did not express confidence in God's goodness. I was not acting as if I believed that God loves me and uses all circumstances for my good. My speech loudly proclaimed what I really believed. *God is not in control of things. If he is, he certainly isn't good. At the very least, I don't like what he is doing, and therefore I have every right to complain and grumble.*

God's View of Grumbling

Paul opens 1 Corinthians 10 by warning his readers not to make the same mistakes the Israelites made. He exhorts us to resist evil desire, forsake idolatry, and avoid sexual immorality. Then he surprisingly adds these words, do not "grumble, as some of them did and were destroyed by the Destroyer" (1 Corinthians 10:10).

We all agree that sins like sexual immorality and idolatry are serious. We agree that they deserve judgment. But *grumbling*? Come on? However, grumbling has a biblical history. God actually destroyed the Jews for this sin. To emphasize this truth Paul concludes, "These things happened to [the Jews] as an example, but they were written down for our instruction" (1 Corinthians 10:11). In other words, God destroyed the Old Testament grumblers so that we would never forget how much God hates this sin. To appreciate the significance of this warning we need to think back on Israel's experience in the wilderness.

The Miracle of the Exodus

The Book of Exodus opens with the Jewish people enslaved by the Egyptians. They cried out to God for deliverance, and he delivered them through a series of plague-judgments that slowly escalated in intensity and pain. This was a massive display of supernatural power. Few have been privileged to witness what Israel saw. To whom much is given much will be expected (Luke 12:48).

The tenth plague was decisive. God sent the angel of death to every firstborn child, but in his kindness he provided a way out for the Jews. God told the Jews that if they killed a lamb and smeared its blood over their doorposts, the angel of death would "pass over" their house. In essence the blood said to the angel, "Please accept the death of this lamb as a substitute for the death of my firstborn son." The blood was a confession. It said,

"In his goodness God has provided a substitute. He will take the blood of the lamb instead of my firstborn."

We all know the story. Pharaoh and the Egyptians proudly rejected these instructions, and all their firstborn died. But the firstborn of those who trusted God's promise were untouched. The next day Pharaoh released the Jews to follow Moses into the wilderness.

This story contains two important lessons. First, no one doubted the *existence* of Yahweh. The Egyptians might have thought their gods were greater, but they did not doubt that Israel's God existed and had some degree of supernatural power. Second, God acted out of love for Israel. He showed mercy and grace to a people who only deserved judgment.

The Miracle of the Red Sea

God's supernatural acts on behalf of the Jews were just beginning. A pillar of cloud led them by day. God's glory was in the cloud, and at night his glory appeared as a pillar of fire. Here were visible, physical emblems of God's presence and care in the midst of God's people.

When Pharaoh changed his mind and decided to pursue Israel, the cloud positioned itself as a wall between the Egyptian chariots and God's people. Moses lifted his staff, the Red Sea parted, and the Jews escaped. When the pillar of cloud moved aside, the Egyptians followed, and the waters enveloped Pharaoh's chariots, destroying his army.

This was the second time God demonstrated his

sovereignty and goodness. He demonstrated his love for Israel. He cared for them. He protected them, and he acted on their behalf.

Grumbling and Complaining in Response to Wilderness Testing

The direct route to Canaan went northeast across the top of the Sinai Peninsula. But the pillar of cloud did not lead that way. Instead, it headed southeast into the burning wilderness where the average rainfall is 4 inches per year and the temperature regularly exceeds 100 degrees.

<u>Water at Marah.</u> Several days later God's people arrived at Marah, hot and thirsty, but they could not drink the water because it was bitter. The reader of Scripture expects them to thank God in a spirit of expectant faith. *Based upon the miracles God has already done for us, what wonder will he do now?* But this was not the attitude of the Israelites. Far from it. Instead, "The people grumbled against Moses" (Exodus 15:24).

God knew the water at Marah was bitter. That is why he led them there. He was testing them. Would they trust him? No—they failed the test. They didn't thank or trust him. They only grumbled.

Note the amazing grace of God. He is slow to anger. He restrained his judgments. Despite their unbelief, he purified the water and led them on to the Oasis of Elim.

<u>Food in the wilderness.</u> They had now been in the desert several days, and their food was running out. Again, we might expect God's people to act with faith.

We expect them to reason like this— *We saw the ten plagues. We watched God destroy the Egyptian army at the Red Sea. God miraculously purified the water of Marah. No bread? No problem. We are God's chosen people. He loves us. We have seen his power in action. He has always come through. He has never failed us. We can't wait to see how he will solve this problem.*

But that is not what happened. Instead, "The whole congregation of the people of Israel *grumbled* against Moses and Aaron" (Exodus 16:2). Again, both the unbelief of Israel and God's patience amazes us. God is faithful and generous beyond all reason. Despite their constant grumbling for forty years until they entered the Promised Land, God delivered fresh manna to Israel every morning.

Water at Rephidim. The Israelites' next stop was Rephidim, where things got worse. At Marah there was water, but it was bitter. However, at Rephidim there was no water at all, and they were in a dry, treeless wilderness. Again, this stop on their journey was no accident. God knew there was no water. Just as he led his people to Marah to test them, he led them to Rephidim. Would they respond with faith? Would they be grateful? Would they give thanks? No. Once again Israel failed the test.

Therefore the people quarreled with Moses and said, "Give us water to drink." And Moses said to them, "Why do you quarrel with me? Why do you test the LORD?" But the people thirsted there for water, and the people grumbled against Moses and said, "Why did you bring us up out of Egypt, to kill us and our children and our livestock with thirst?" (Exodus 17:2–3).

Moses struck the rock, and clean, cold water gushed. Paul reminds us that this rock was Christ, and from this point forward he followed Israel through the wilderness dispensing life-giving water (1 Corinthians 10:4). So once again the pattern repeated itself. Israel grumbled and complained, but God responded with kindness, faithfulness, and generosity.

Mount Sinai and departure for Canaan. Finally, Israel arrived at Mount Sinai. There they received God's law, built a tabernacle for God's dwelling place, ordained Aaron and his family into the priesthood, and rested for one year. Meanwhile God fed them with manna and refreshed them with water from the Rock.

However, when Israel departed for Canaan the pattern of grumbling returned. Once more "the people complained in the hearing of the LORD" (Numbers 11:1a). Finally, God's patience ran out. "And when the LORD heard it, his anger was kindled, and the fire of the LORD burned among them and consumed some outlying parts of the camp" (Numbers 11:1b).

Three times the people complained—at Marah, in the wilderness, and at Rephidim—and three times God was amazingly patient. Although God is slow to anger, if continually provoked, his anger will eventually kindle.

Despite God's judgment, Israel's grumbling grew worse.

> And the people of Israel also wept again and said, "Oh that we had meat to eat! We remember the fish we ate in Egypt that cost nothing, the cucumbers, the melons, the leeks, the onions, and the garlic. But now our strength is dried up, and there is nothing at all but this manna to look at" (Numbers 11:4–6).

The reader is astounded. God just consumed them with fire. In addition, he has repeatedly and supernaturally provided them with food and water. Despite this they again responded with grumbling. So God judged them a second time. "The anger of the LORD was kindled against the people, and the LORD struck down the people with a very great plague" (Numbers 11:33–34).

Destroyed by the Destroyer

We have now come to the "destroyer" Paul mentions in 1 Corinthians 10:10. Seeking intelligence about the Land of Promise, Moses sent out twelve spies. Ten returned in unbelief. Again, we are amazed that God's people have apparently forgotten their deliverance from Pharaoh, forgotten the parting of the Red Sea, forgotten the destruction of six hundred chariots, forgotten the waters of Marah made sweet, forgotten the manna, and forgotten the crystal-pure water gushing from the rock. They have forgotten that God is both good and sovereign. "We came to the land to which you sent us," the spies reported. "It flows with milk and honey, and this is its fruit. However, the people who dwell in the land are strong, and the cities are fortified and very large. And besides, we saw the descendants of Anak there" (Numbers 13:27–28).

The spies did not trust God. Most significantly, Israel listened to them.

> And all the people of Israel *grumbled* against Moses and Aaron…"Would that we had died in the land of Egypt! Or would that we had died in this wilderness…Would it not be better for us to go back to Egypt?" And they said to one another, "Let us choose a leader and go back to Egypt" (Numbers 14:2–4).

As we saw in chapter one, Israel's grumbling cast aspersions on God's glory. It said "God is not good. He cannot be trusted. He is not sovereign." And that is exactly how God saw it.

> The LORD said to Moses, "How long will this people *despise* me? And how long will they not believe in me, *in spite of all the signs that I have done among them?* I will strike them with the pestilence and disinherit them, and I will make of you a nation greater and mightier than they" (Numbers 14:11–12).

Moses responded to God's threat with love for the Israelites. He interceded. He asked God to have mercy on them. God relented and didn't destroy the nation. However, because Israel had just complained, "Would that we had *died in this wilderness* rather than face the giants in the Land of Promise," God let them have what they asked for.

> And your children shall be shepherds in the wilderness forty years and shall suffer for your faithlessness, until the last of your dead bodies lies in the wilderness. According to the number of the days in which you spied out the land, forty days, a year for each day, you shall bear your iniquity forty years, and you shall know my displeasure (Numbers 14:33–34).

All of this is what Paul had in mind when he wrote his crucial warning in 1 Corinthians 10:10 "Nor grumble as some of them did and were destroyed by the Destroyer."

The destroyer was not the Devil. The Destroyer was the Angel of the Lord, an agent of God himself!

Three Lessons about Grumbling

We can draw three important lessons from this story.

<u>Grumbling equals despising.</u> First, no Christian would ever think of himself as despising God, but that is exactly how God sees grumbling and complaining. It

is synonymous to despising him. "How long will this people despise me? And how long will they not believe in me, in spite of all the signs that I have done among them?" (Numbers 14:11). Why are *grumbling* and *despising* synonyms? Because our grumbling, complaining, and whining reveal a heart-level conviction that God is either not fully good, not fully sovereign, not fully trustworthy, or all three.

Grumbling is an open window through which God and others can view the arrogance of the complainer's heart. At that moment, he or she is actually looking down on God and assuming a position of superiority. Such complaining says, "If God were truly wise and loving, he would treat me better." This is why God calls it the sin of despising him. When we despise God we rob him of his rightful glory, praise, and worship.

We are accountable to the extent of our privileges. Second, in light of what God had allowed Israel to see and experience, their behavior was inexcusable. They had witnessed amazing demonstrations of God's supernatural power, grace, and love, yet they still failed to trust him. Jesus repeatedly stressed the truth that God holds us accountable according to the privileges we have experienced (Luke 12:47–48; Matthew 12:41). This explains why Israel's judgments were so severe.

Grumbling is a heart issue. That brings us to our third lesson. Miracles, by themselves, will never convince us that God is trustworthy (see Luke 16:19–

31). The Jews saw amazing miracles, but failed to trust.
How can this be? Because they lacked the conviction
about God's goodness that can only come from new
birth.

The Ultimate Reason for Gratitude

Clearly, we need something more than the experience
of miracles. In order to trust God we need a spiritual
heart-transplant. This is why Ezekiel prophesied that
in the New Covenant God's Spirit would remove our
hearts of stone and replace them with hearts of flesh
(Ezekiel 36:26). The Old and New Testaments both
call this a circumcised heart. Jesus calls it the new birth.
It is a growing disposition to love God and obey him
because we are convinced he is good.

Because they saw mighty miracles, Israel believed
that God existed. They probably believed that he was
omnipotent, certainly more powerful than Egypt's
gods. But without the new birth they lacked the confidence in his goodness that produces the trust which, in
turn, motivates obedience. People who do not believe
that God is good will not trust him. And people who
do not trust God will not obey him. Israel lacked this
confidence, and that is why they continually grumbled.

Even in adverse circumstances, a person with true,
saving faith rests confident in God's goodness. Faith in
God produces trust in God, and by the exercise of that
trust we are able to conquer grumbling and self-pity

with thanksgiving. This is the connection between the new birth and an increasing capacity for gratitude in both bad times and good.

However, even with the new birth our confidence in his goodness is imperfect. It needs to grow, so where do we go to get more? We go back to the cross—the essential resource that Israel lacked. Those who meditate on the cross experience the knowledge of God's goodness that was withheld from Israel. Indeed, the cross displays the goodness of God like no other event in history. The cross is the ultimate reason to trust him, and therefore the ultimate rationale for a life overflowing with thanksgiving and gratitude.

Think about it. At the cross God's Son gave himself up to death by slow, excruciating torture. He absorbed the wrath you and I deserve. He didn't do this for friends. He did it for *enemies* (Romans 5:10). He suffered this way for creatures he does not need, creatures that can add nothing to his happiness, creatures that deserve nothing but the wrath of divine justice. This is amazing love. This is off-the-charts goodness. The apostle Paul calls it "love that surpasses knowledge" (Ephesians 3:19). At the cross God's Son showed us what cosmic goodness looks like, and it is utterly astounding. It jams the hard drives of our imaginations.

God will hold Christians accountable for this knowledge. We have a greater responsibility to overflow with thanksgiving than did Israel. "Everyone to whom much was given, of him much will be required, and from him to whom they entrusted much, they will demand the more" (Luke 12:48). This is why Paul's "destroyer" warning in 1 Corinthians 10 is real, and solemn, and applies to you and me just as it did to the Corinthians.

Israel enjoyed a limited knowledge of God's goodness, but we don't have that excuse. The cross of Christ confronts us with the most astounding display of divine goodness in history. God wants us to fear God. He wants us to learn from Israel's experience, meditate on the cross, and increasingly jettison grumbling, complaining, and self-pity.

We can learn another lesson from Israel's experience. If God tested the Israelites with trouble and scarcity, he will also test us. Just as God led the nation of Israel into the wilderness, the Holy Spirit led Jesus into the wilderness to be tempted by the Devil (Matthew 4:1). Note: God did not tempt Jesus. The Devil tempted Jesus, but the Holy Spirit led Jesus into the wilderness, to a place of great scarcity, so that he could be tempted. It was God's will that Jesus endure temptation. In the same way, God will lead us into our own personal wildernesses to be tempted. How will we respond? Will we overflow with thanksgiving to the glory of God? Will our gratitude say to those watching that God is infinitely good, that he can be trusted in both good times and bad?

The truth is, we often fail these trials. Instead of

trusting God, we all too easily complain and grumble. All of us have despised God this way. (Think of my temper tantrum when my hard drive failed.) Indeed, some of us have been tempted to resent God for the tests he brings—a child near death; repeated surgeries without improved health; a time of protracted unemployment; a failing grade at school; a painful, unhappy marriage, or _____ (fill in the blank). Like Israel, our grumbling deserves judgment. We deserve a visit from the Destroyer.

And now it is time for us to think again about God's goodness. Despite the reality of what our grumbling deserves, the astounding fact is this—Jesus stepped forward to be judged and punished for our grumbling! He took the punishment that our whining deserves. He took it for everyone who will trust him for salvation.

Here's how it works. When we become Christians, God imputes all of the guilt for our complaining and grumbling to Christ. God assigns it to him. The reverse also happens: God imputes all of Christ's trust and gratitude to you and me! Despite our constant tendency to grumble, the Father forgives us and clothes us in (that is, he imputes to us) his Son's perfect trust, gratitude, and resulting praise. Summed up, Jesus took the punishment that our complaining deserves so that we could enjoy the reward that his perfect gratitude deserves. Amazing!

Picture of Perfect Gratitude

In the area of gratitude, none of us measure up. Therefore Jesus' gratitude is utterly crucial. Jesus is a portrait of what a grateful life is supposed to look like. He obeyed all of the Old Testament injunctions to rejoice and be thankful. He did this because of his profound confidence in his Father's sovereignty and goodness.

The evidence for Christ's gratitude is abundant. The Bible tells us that Jesus perfectly fulfilled God's law, that he was the only sinless man (Hebrews 4:15; 1 Peter 2:22). This means he obeyed all of God's Old Testament commands including the many exhortations to be grateful and give thanks (Psalm 100:4; 118:1, 29; 50:14, 23 are examples). Scripture specifically describes him thanking his Father for concealing and revealing truth (Matthew 11:25), for providing bread to feed thousands (Matthew 15:36), for making bread and wine available for the Last Supper (Matthew 26:27), and for hearing his earnest prayers to raise Lazarus from the dead (John 11:41). But most importantly, he thanked his Father in times of great suffering and need.

A few moments before his death on the cross Jesus cried out "My God, my God, why have you forsaken me?" (Matthew 27:46). This was a direct quote from Psalm 22:1. That Psalm predicted the agonies of Christ's crucifixion and subsequent victory, and for the next few verses it allows us to read Christ's thoughts in his hour of cosmic suffering. "Why are you so far from saving me, from the words of my groaning? O my God, I cry by day, but you do not answer, and by night, but I find no rest" (vv 1–2). Jesus felt utterly forsaken and abandoned. He was tempted to despair. His body was wracked with pain. It would be hard to imagine feeling lower.

Despite this, he put his thoughts on God. "Yet you are holy, enthroned on the praises of Israel. In you our fathers *trusted*; they *trusted*, and you delivered them. To you they cried and were rescued; in you they *trusted* and were not put to shame" (vv 3–5). Jesus remembers the many times that the Jewish fathers trusted God and were grateful. Think of the heroes of faith in Hebrews 11. Noah built an ark, Abraham left his home, Moses led the Exodus, the prophets spoke with great courage, and more. However, Jesus is not saying that the Jewish fathers trusted God perfectly. In light of their wilderness wanderings, we know they did not. Grumbling, a fruit of unbelief, characterized the Jews, and this sin needed to be atoned for.

Therefore, in circumstances much worse than anything Israel had ever faced, Jesus does the one thing Israel did not—*he trusts God perfectly*. In fact, in verses 3–5 Christ refers to trust three times. At the point of absolute despair he rests in God's goodness. He *trusts* God for the outcome. He remembers God's faithfulness to Israel. He reminds himself that God is both sovereign and good. He *chooses* to trust. Despite his terrible circumstance Christ "enthrones God on his praises." In this context, praise and thanksgiving are synonyms.

Psalm 69 also prophesies Christ's suffering and

death (vv 4, 9, 21, 22). The New Testament writers cite it four times. All four confirm that the person suffering in this Psalm is the Messiah. He is in mortal agony. He is like Jonah on the bottom of the sea. But then comes verse 30, "I will praise the name of God with song; I will magnify him with thanksgiving."

Jesus triumphed where you and I routinely fail, and we should be thankful. That is because God imputes Christ's amazing gratitude to all who believe the gospel. Without it you will not get into heaven. God imputes Christ's thankfulness to those who deserve judgment for their grumbling. All this further amplifies our conviction that God is good and we can trust him. And so God uses our failings and God's mercy for good. Confronted by the amazing grace of God, our sins make us even more grateful.

Gratitude When Tested

For these reasons the cross is the decisive reason to trust God. The cross is the ultimate rationale for a life over-flowing with thanksgiving. The cross is also our hope when we doubt his goodness, when we fail to trust him, and when we respond to his tests with grumbling, self-pity, and whining.

When we are tested with pain and trouble, when problems tempt us to doubt God's goodness and sovereignty, run to the cross. The cross reminds us that God is infinitely good. Where Israel failed to trust God and thank him, Jesus triumphed.

When my hard drive went down I failed the test. I didn't respond with heart-felt thanks. I complained. I deserved a visit from the Destroyer. However, he didn't come. Figuratively, Jesus stepped forward to be destroyed in my place. That is what the cross is all about. He took the judgment my complaining deserves so that I could experience the reward his gratitude deserves. On the basis of this transaction God forgives this grumbler.

In the end, God used my sinful grumbling for good. God used his response of grace to my failure to heighten my awareness of his love, and that in turn made me more grateful. It motivated me to thank him even more. It increased my capacity to trust him. The cross turned my grumbling into thanksgiving. The cross is why Paul continually exhorts us to overflow with thanksgiving. Cross-centered Christians understand this. They increasingly trust God, and gratitude is the overflow.

So let us "enter his gates with thanksgiving" (Psalm 100:4). Let us "give thanks in all circumstances" (1 Thessalonians 5:18). Let us be "abounding in thanksgiving" (Colossians 2:7). Finally, let us give "thanks always and for everything to God the Father in the Name of our Lord Jesus Christ" (Ephesians 5:20). Amen!

Four
STRIKING BACK
AT SELF-PITY

Thousands of villagers in India have experienced the nightmare of slow, invisible poisoning. Their well water contains trace amounts of arsenic. Because arsenic is colorless and tasteless, they have no way of detecting it. And since it comes in such minute quantities, the negative effects appear gradually, over years.

The first outward manifestation is melanosis, or dark spots on the chest, back, limbs, and gums. Continual poisoning by arsenic results in enlargement of the liver, kidneys, and spleen, as well as gangrene, and cancers of the lung, skin, and bladder.[12] At low concentration levels, it takes between eight and fourteen years for the physical symptoms to emerge. By then it is often too late.

Self-pity is a spiritual poison that is similar to arsenic. When persistently indulged in it can destroy the soul and, like arsenic poisoning, the damage can go undetected for years. Self-pity is an assassin of spiritual joy! To you and me, however, self-pity can seem so innocuous, so reasonable. It feels like a normal reaction to disappointment or trouble. Yet as Richard Smith points out,

> [Self-pity] is to be resisted with every fiber of your being...We are bombarded with opportunities to feel sorry for ourselves. Every day we are misunderstood, overworked, underappreciated, and even abused, and regularly "something unfair" will happen: we will become ill, miss a train. We may even suspect a conspiracy: "somebody's out to get me."[13]

That "somebody" that will "get me" is myself, drenched in self-pity. This sin comes in many forms. Consider these composite examples.

- After twenty years of marriage, Betty's husband left her for a younger, more beautiful woman. She became depressed, morose, self-obsessed, and bitter toward God. Most significantly, she indulged in self-pity. *I deserve better,* she reasoned.
- Jack felt dejected. He had been married to Joanne for thirty years. Their children were raised, and he and Joanne had retired early to enjoy their "golden years." But those years were not turning out to be golden. He had colon cancer, and Jack was now staring down the long barrel of chemotherapy

with no guarantee of recovery. Withdrawing from family and friends, he brooded over his "bad luck." He refused to respond with gratitude. Instead, he spiraled deeper and deeper into an abyss of self-pity.

- A truck rear-ended Fred's Honda Civic, breaking his back. Out of work for three months, he was now living with chronic pain. *Why me?*, he angrily wondered. He envied healthy people, and became more and more depressed as he descended into a vortex of self-pity.

Few recognize the pervasive nature of self-pity — it really is all about *self*. A wife pities herself for the lack of sexual intimacy in her marriage. A man pouts because he did not get the promotion he surely deserves. Paul Mizzi notes that "All problems that can be dealt with and solved in Christian counseling sessions are always due to the pride, self-centeredness, [or the] self-pity of the counselee."[14]

Self-pity is spiritual poison.

The Nature of Self-Pity

What is self-pity? What is its nature and character?

<u>Self-pity is delusional in nature.</u> Pride is spiritual blindness. It is the inability to see myself for who I really am in relation to God and other men and women. Pride is a hyper-inflated view of self.

By contrast, the real truth about ourselves is

profoundly humbling. I am a hopelessly flawed sinner in desperate need of God's grace. I deserve nothing from God but judgment. This means I am much more flawed than I think. But it also means I am much more loved by God than I have any reason to think.

Self-pity rejects these truths. It says, "I am a good person, at least as good as average, and God loves me *because* I am good." The banner over self-pity is, "I deserve! I deserve!" Self-pity is deeply anchored in the pride that is foundational to our fallen natures.

Self-pity is angry and self-destructive. "I can't believe God (or fate or bad luck) did this to me!" A garbage truck runs over the neighbor's cat, and its owner shakes her fist at God. She is angry. She deserves better. A teen track star drowns, and his father descends into self-pity. He refuses to discuss the accident or his son. He is angry at Christians and the God they worship. He walls off the world and retreats into his own personal hell.

Self-pity is an expression of self-centeredness. It is a magnifying glass turned inward upon me and my problems. It typically has little energy for God, little interest in the needs of others, and little capacity for the outward focus that signals spiritual health and produces true happiness. Self-pity is all about me and my entitlements. Society owes me. God owes me. Life owes me. Victim-hood is the trough in which self-pity wallows.

Self-pity is self-worship. Here is what really makes self-pity so deadly, so lethal. At heart, it is simply the worship of self. Self demands center stage. Self elevates my personal needs to the highest priority. Self seeks to be worshipped, dethroning even God himself.

The Symptoms of Self-Pity

Because it is delusional, self-pity is ugly. It is frequently obvious to others, but often the person himself has difficulty recognizing it. Like arsenic poisoning, those snared in self-pity are often completely unaware. Close attention to the following symptoms, however, can help us detect it in ourselves before it spreads too far.

Depression. Depression is often the first symptom of self-pity. Some find perverse joy in the gloominess of feeling sorry for themselves. It can feel so good to feel so bad. There is a reason for this depression. Christians gain their lives by losing them (Matthew 16:25), but you *can't* gain your life by losing it when you are gripping it with all your strength.

Sometimes when someone says, "I am depressed," they are really saying, "I'm feeling sorry for myself." They might even say, "I'm completely worn out when I get up, and I'm worn out when I go to bed." Often self-pity is the debilitating, underlying culprit.

Envy. Envy is another symptom of self-pity. "I *want* what you have" is at the heart of it. This same general attitude can also express itself through the resentment of jealousy, i.e. "I *deserve* what you have."

When God accepted Abel's offering but rejected Cain's, Cain envied his brother. He should have

69

rejoiced in his brother's success, but instead Cain became jealous, believing that he deserved the same good treatment his brother was getting. In his anger and self-pity, he plotted against his brother and killed him (Genesis 4:5–8).

Anger. Sinful anger is another symptom of self-pity. "He or she is an angry, envious person," notes Jay Adams, "bewailing bitterly the good deals others get in contrast to what has been meted out to him or her."[15] Sinful anger erupts when I want something but can't have it. It rains down its ugly debris on those closest to me.

Bitterness. Bitterness is likewise a symptom of self-pity. It may often appear to be directed toward other people, but the ultimate target is always God. "If God was really good, my spouse would not have left me…I would be married by now…I would have the grace to overcome gluttony, or smoking, or gossip, or _____."

Is anything more counterintuitive than bitterness toward God? Think about it. He holds all the cards. He made you from nothing and breathed into your soul the breath of life. He gave his Son for you. If you are his creature, and God is your Creator, you have no "rights." Every breath is a gift. You belong to your Creator. David's cry, "What is man that you are mindful of him?" (Psalm 8:4), should constantly humble us.

Pouting. King Ahab desperately wanted Naboth's

vineyard, but Naboth refused to sell it to him. So "Ahab went into his house vexed and sullen because of what Naboth the Jezreelite had said to him…And he lay down on his bed and turned away his face and would eat no food" (1 Kings 21:4).

Here is a textbook description of self-pity: vexed, sullen, face-to-the-wall, not eating. He is pouting. Ahab wanted Naboth's vineyard. He felt entitled to it but couldn't have it, so he withdrew into self-pity. Ahab's self-pity led to even more serious sin. Jezebel, Ahab's wife, manipulated his self-pity, initiating a scheme that, coupled with other sins, ended in Naboth's murder.

"Out of the abundance of the heart the mouth speaks" (Matthew 12:34). Eventually a heart saturated in self-pity will express itself through depression, envy, jealousy, anger, bitterness, or pouting.

Self-Pity and the Cross

I recently heard about a Vietnam vet who lost both legs to a Claymore mine. As he lay recovering in a veterans' hospital, self-pity completely controlled him. One day his nurse wheeled him into an adjoining ward. There he saw a man whose face was burnt off and another who had lost all four limbs. One patient had lost his sight and hearing, and some were completely paralyzed. The contrast between his problems and theirs completely changed his perspective. He returned to his ward filled with gratitude for how good he had it.

In a sense, the cross wheels us into an adjoining ward. But the cross exceeds this illustration in two ways. It shows us severe suffering of a kind that we as Christians will never experience. And it shows what we actually *deserve*.

The Son of God, dying as our *substitute*, endured the wrath of God that each of us personally deserve. The cross therefore proclaims a profound reason to abandon self-pity: not only *will I never* experience what Jesus suffered, I actually *deserve* to experience what he suffered, and I deserve to suffer it *forever*.

The cross also shows us four other truths. Each one seriously undermines the grounds of self-pity.

The cross shows how much God hates all sin. This applies especially to the sin of self-pity. On the cross Jesus absorbed the wrath that our self-pity deserves along with all the pride that fuels it. That is how serious self-pity is—the appropriate punishment is death by crucifixion. Few of us see it this way. We take "feeling sorry for ourselves" lightly. In fact, we usually feel justified to wallow in it for a while. *Certainly God doesn't mind*, we reason. *After all, I deserve to feel sorry for myself.* But anyone who sees his own self-pity through the lens of the cross will see it as God sees it. He will hate it. He will increasingly detest this sin and seek to turn from it whole-heartedly.

The cross proclaims God's amazing love. There on the cross, Jesus Christ endured the wrath my self-pity deserves. Why? Because he loves me. He is passionately committed to my eternal happiness. This is an astounding truth. Jesus took the wrath my self-pity deserves so that I can inherit the eternal reward his perfect gratitude deserves. This truth can have a dramatic effect on my tendency to self-pity. When I see the extravagant nature of God's love for me, despite this sin, how can my self-pity not yield to thanksgiving?

The cross models what gratitude is supposed to look like. God created us to live in constant gratitude and joy, despite our circumstances. Jesus, the only sinless man, showed us what this looks like. As we saw in the previous chapter, he is the only person who has ever deserved nothing but good from God, yet God sent him to the cross for our sins. The only man who had a right to pity himself *didn't*. Instead, he was too busy praying for his tormentors to feel sorry for himself.

Faith in the cross frees us from the penalty this ugly sin deserves. Here is the astounding, earth-shaking nature of God's love. He imputes our self-pity to Jesus. The Son of God receives the wrath we deserve. Then God imputes Christ's perfect gratitude to us, and we receive the reward that his infinite gratitude deserves.

Conquering Self-Pity

Given all that we have learned so far, how can we escape the clutches of self-pity? How can we, instead, put on the heart of joy and gratitude extolled in the first chapter? And how can we help those burdened by self-pity — men and women like Betty, Jack, and Fred — to apply the cross? Here are some suggestions.

Begin with repentance. God is rich in mercy. Because of the cross, he will forgive liberally. So repent of this sin, then turn from it by cultivating the discipline of a grateful heart. Start by practicing thanksgiving for trivial things — hot coffee, warm blankets, family, a job, political freedom, central heat, a smart phone, and so much more.

Put your eyes on the cross of Christ. Let its truths humble you. Confess what you really deserve and rejoice that, at Christ's expense, you will never get it. Christ died in your place. As we have seen, he took the punishment you deserve so that he could give you the reward he deserves. Continuously and repeatedly wheel yourself, and those you serve, into the adjoining ward where the truth of the cross puts our problems in proper perspective.

Here is an example of how the cross helped a friend.

Joe's marriage was in trouble. He complained about his wife, Mandy. She was attractive, cheerful, and amiable in public, and their children were well-behaved. But Joe was distressed. She did not listen to him. She did not satisfy his sexual needs. She did not clean the house adequately. She did not encourage or submit to his leadership. In short, she was a "high-maintenance" woman. He deserved better, and he was angry and depressed because he wasn't getting it. Joe displayed many of the symptoms of self-pity.

Some of Joe's complaints were valid, yet he was blind to Mandy's positive qualities, and she had many. To Joe, Mandy was a glass half-empty. I knew that the message of the cross was the place to begin solving their marital problems.

"I feel compassion for your marital stress. I know you are suffering, and I want to help. I want to share some advice, but I need to warn you that it is going to be counterintuitive. Are you open?"

"Yes. What's your advice?"

"God wants you to be grateful for Mandy."

Joe looked at me like I had hit him with a stun gun.

"I am not saying she doesn't need to change in some ways. What I am saying is that, in light of the inherent sinfulness of every human being, your marriage should actually be much worse. The cross says that you and Mandy both deserve crucifixion. So the best way to begin healing your marriage is to meditate on God's incredible mercy. Your wife loves you, your children are healthy, you have a good job, and God has given you saving faith. Shouldn't you be thankful? I know Mandy is imperfect. I know there are problems. I know she needs to change, and we will work on those changes later, but in light of what you deserve, your marriage is not a glass half-empty. It is a glass half-full. Can you relate to this?"

Joe listened carefully. Then he asked, "We deserve

crucifixion? I don't understand what you mean. How does that apply to my problems?"

I was thankful for his honesty. Joe spoke for many Christians. I have learned never to assume that a Christian adequately understands the gospel. Although Joe had been a Christian for many years, the message of the cross had not fully penetrated. Yes, he believed that Jesus died for him. He understood that he was saved by faith alone. But what the cross said about his sin and what he truly deserved had not moved from his mind to his heart. There was a disconnect for Joe, something common among believers.

I wanted Joe to know that step one in healing his marriage was not to help Mandy change. That would come later. Undoubtedly Joe needed to change as well, but before that could happen he needed a new perspective—one that would help him see his own sin more clearly. So the first requirement for Joe was an infusion of self-pity-slaying gratitude. He needed to see his sin and what it deserves. He needed a fresh, penetrating view of the cross and all that it says about Joe and his sin.

I explained to Joe the four truths about the cross mentioned above. He agreed to go home and think about them. As he began to see how they applied to him personally, he was humbled by the cross and began to be grateful. Over the next few months he became increasingly thankful for Mandy. His growing humility opened his eyes to her strengths. Other changes followed. As Joe changed, Mandy noticed and began to respond. Today their marriage is greatly improved.

Besides repenting and focusing on the cross there is one last thing we can do to conquer self-pity.

Focus on eternity. No matter how great this life's suffering, it is short compared to the infinite, eternal happiness awaiting those who persevere in faith. When the inevitable trials come and the temptation to self-pity follows, meditate on passages like 2 Corinthians 4:16–5:5. Remind yourself that, as an adopted child of God, eternal glory is your heritage. Saturate yourself and others in this perspective. Fire your imagination with hope and gratitude. Remember that, for the joy set before him, Christ endured the cross (Hebrews 12:2). For Jesus, the glass was always half-full—at the end of the day there was a rainbow; on the other side of the injustice of the cross was resurrection life and eternal reward.

This is not about putting on a Pollyanna happy-face and pretending we have no struggles. Gratitude does not always bring instant improvement in our souls. Sometimes we will find ourselves outwardly expressing gratitude when inside we actually feel sorrow, fear, anxiety, or depression. A true confession of biblical gratitude may not always express our feelings, but it will always express our faith. Nevertheless, whatever our emotional state, we can give thanks because we *believe* what the cross teaches about ourselves and God.

Conclusion

Don't allow the poison of self-pity to slowly kill your spiritual joy. In the short run self-pity feels good, but it is really spiritual arsenic.

Self-pity is characterized by spiritual delusion, angry self-destruction, selfishness, and idolatry. Its symptoms include depression, envy, jealousy, anger, bitterness, and pouting.

Take God's antidote for self-pity—the work of Christ on the cross. Meditate on the cross. Humble yourself under God's mighty hand. Remember what you deserve. See self-pity as God sees it, nailed to the cross. Meditate on what the cross says about the Father's infinite personal love for *you*. Meditate on Jesus. When treated unjustly, he refused to yield to self-pity or complaining. Instead, he gave thanks.

As you meditate on the cross, a self-pity-slaying gratitude will increasingly flow, and a heaven-sent spiritual joy will increasingly replace it.

Five

THE SECRET OF SPIRITUAL JOY

The most important question for an author to answer is the "so what?" question. Now that you've spent four chapters learning how to speak the language of humility, celebrate a sovereign and good God, get a grip on grumbling, and strike back at your own self-pity, what does it all mean? How can all this make a difference in your life, and what can you do to help make that happen? The purpose of this final chapter is to answer these questions.

God motivates the saints by convincing us that both his person and his commands exist for our ultimate good. This is the faith-conviction that ultimately conquers worldly temptation. To the degree that each believer is really convinced that his ultimate happiness is intimately bound up in knowing and obeying Jesus Christ, he will pursue God and obey him. That is the purpose of this last chapter. I want to convince you that your happiness is tied to cultivating the discipline of thanksgiving. It is the secret of spiritual joy!

In other words, the secret is learning to overflow with gratitude (Colossians 2:7). The Christian who internalizes the discipline of gratitude will reap benefits in at least eight areas of spiritual growth. These areas will be our focus in this final chapter.

Humility

Grateful Christians are increasingly humble. Indeed, a heart overflowing with gratitude does two things. It *expresses* humility, and it also helps one *grow* in humility.

Words of gratitude not only reveal what is in the heart. They are also the rudder that guides the heart (James 3:4–5). The words we think or speak change us, for good or for ill. "Gratitude is a revealer of the heart, not just a reporter of details," notes Nancy Leigh DeMoss. "And among the things it reveals about us most is our level of humility."[16] DeMoss is right. There is a profound connection between gratitude and humility. We already touched on this subject in chapter one. We noted that humility is essential to Christianity. It attracts God's favor. It is the virtue from which all other virtues spring. It is essential to godliness. I wrote *Gospel Powered Humility* to defend this idea in detail.[17]

So what is the connection between gratitude and humility? Out of the heart the mouth speaks. Words of gratitude confess our creatureliness. They confess our dependency. God is the giver, and I am the receiver. God needs nothing that I can give to him. "Who has given a gift to him that he might be repaid?" (Romans 11:35). Answer: no one! By contrast, I am totally needy. I need him for every breath, every friend, every bite of food, and every advance in life.

Words of gratitude say that God is in charge, and I am not. In his scholarly book on thanksgiving David Pao writes, "When God is acknowledged as the Lord of all, thanksgiving becomes a *humbling act* admitting the dependency of human existence."[18] In fact, Pao notes that for the early church fathers dependency was what thanksgiving was really all about.[19]

Let's assume I am having issues with someone and don't know how to fix them. I have done everything God asks, but the problems persists. Thanksgiving confesses to God that he has known about these situations from before the foundation of the world, that in fact he ordered these circumstances in part to mature me, and that despite these problems I will never get what I deserve (eternity in hell). Thanksgiving also confesses that God is good, that he alone knows the solution, and that he will reveal it in his time.

Grumbling, complaining, and self-pity express the opposite. They express pride. The proud man actually thinks he is autonomous, or at least that he should be. He is a man who craves independence, with no need of God or others. He is the silent, independent, and self-sufficient loner, the James Bond of the Christian life. In addition, he usually thinks he deserves better than he is getting. He has not been humbled by the reality of the cross. That is why DeMoss writes, "Pride is the father of ingratitude and the silent killer of gratitude. We think we deserve so much."[20] A person who is convinced that he or she deserves *better* than they are getting will never be thankful for what they *are* getting. Just the opposite. They will grumble and complain.

When you humble yourself with thanksgiving, you let thanksgiving have its humbling effect on your heart. The tongue is the rudder. The more we speak words of gratitude and thanksgiving, the more we feel the humility that gratitude expresses.

Meekness

Grateful Christians are increasingly meek. Words of heartfelt gratitude also express and advance a virtue that is closely related to humility—meekness. Meekness is the ability to respond to troubles and unexpected events with serenity and composure. Meekness expresses deep faith and trust in God.

When our children were little we took them camping. In the middle of the night it started to rain. We were miserable. Then it got worse: four of the kids suddenly got sick with a flu virus and began to throw up all over the inside of the tent! I'm going to go easy on myself here and simply say that I didn't respond with meekness. I should have. But I was not thankful, and I was not grateful. If I had understood *and applied* what I have written so far in this book, I would have at least *tried* to be thankful. Simply making the effort would have flavored my outward demeanor with meekness—to my family's immense relief. But I didn't do that, and in the morning we folded up our camping gear in the rain and drove home wet, sick, and miserable, our vacation ruined.

By contrast, Jonathan Edwards (1703–1758) was a model of meekness. Most consider him North America's greatest theologian. Despite this, and for petty reasons, in 1750 his Massachusetts congregation fired him. He had been their pastor for more than twenty years. He was in his late forties, with a large family, no other job prospects, and no ability to do anything but preach and write. Most people in a similar situation would respond with self-pity and worry, or worse.

Instead, Edwards responded with meekness. Here is how a fellow minister described Jonathan during the week of his trial by the church council that eventually dismissed him. "I never saw the least symptoms of displeasure in his countenance the whole week, but he appeared like a man of God, *whose happiness was out of the reach of his enemies*, and whose treasure was not only a future but a present good, overbalancing all imaginable ills of life, even to the astonishment of many, who could not be at rest without his dismission."[21] Edwards' reaction to their rejection is a picture of biblical meekness.

Meekness flows from a heart disciplined by the

daily expression of gratitude for everything (Colossians 3:17). It is the outward demeanor of a heart at rest, a heart confident in God's goodness and sovereignty. I don't know anyone who doesn't want a large dose of Edwards' meekness. According to those watching, it put him "out of the reach of his enemies," and so it will do for us.

Because gratitude is at the root of meekness, it also prepares us to rule. "Blessed are the meek, for they shall inherit the earth" (Matthew 5:5). Again, gratitude expresses faith. It says, "My confidence is in God." A thankful heart sees beyond the pain of the moment to God's sovereign hand working all things together for its good. A grateful heart is the father of meekness.

Contentment

Grateful Christians are increasingly content. Not surprisingly, contentment is closely related to humility and meekness. Expressed negatively, contentment is the absence of covetousness. "You shall not covet your neighbor's house; you shall not covet your neighbor's wife, or his male servant, or his female servant, or his ox, or his donkey, or anything that is your neighbor's" (Exodus 20:17).

Positively, contentment is the ability to embrace the fact of our needs with the joy that only a grateful heart can produce.

Covetous people are unhappy people. They are restless and dissatisfied. They are complainers and grumblers full of self-pity. They are unable to find peace in the moment. I want that promotion, that new couch, a larger home in a nicer neighborhood, or a more prestigious car. You fill in the blank. It is different for each of us, for our hearts are naturally covetous and endlessly grasping.

Judas suffered from covetousness. He was unable to be grateful for his financial condition. He stole from the money bag that supported Jesus and the disciples. By contrast, Paul learned contentment in every circumstance (Philippians 4:11). This included his finances. It is no accident that, more than any other biblical writer, he also exhorted his followers to a life of gratitude and thanksgiving.

Thanksgiving is the fountain of contentment and the cure for covetousness. *God, I am so thankful for my station in life, for what you have given and what you have not given, for my possessions and all that I have received from your gracious hand.* Every expression of gratitude weakens the pride that powers covetousness. Words of heartfelt gratitude are knockout blows, sending the enemy reeling onto the ropes of defeat.

These first three fruits—humility, meekness, and contentment—are an appeal to our natural desire for happiness. To the degree that we possess these fruits we will be happy. The person with the opposites—pride, self-will, and covetousness—will be unhappy. Holy people are happy people. To the degree we are unholy, we will be unhappy. Gratitude is a fruit of holiness. Therefore, a grateful, thankful heart is foundational to true happiness. If for no other reason than your happiness, cultivate the discipline of thanksgiving.

Worship

Grateful Christians are the worshipers God seeks. Throughout the Bible, praise and thanksgiving are closely related. In fact, sometimes the Bible uses them nearly as synonyms. Here are just a few examples.

> I will praise the name of God with a song; I will magnify him with thanksgiving (Psalm 69:30).

> Let us come into his presence with thanksgiving; let us make a joyful noise to him with songs of praise! (Psalm 95:2).

> Enter his gates with thanksgiving, and his courts with praise! (Psalm 100:4).

> I give you thanks, O LORD, with my whole heart; before the gods I sing your praise (Psalm 138:1).

When the fire of God fell on Solomon's temple-sacrifice the people "worshipped and gave thanks" (2 Chronicles 7:3). The two always go together. In fact, one of the most effective ways to enter into worship is to begin with thanksgiving. Thanksgiving will morph into praise, and praise into heart-felt worship. It would be no exaggeration to say that every time a believer lifts up his or her heart to God in thanksgiving, God gets the worship and praise that pleases him. "Thanksgiving in Paul *is an act of worship,*" notes David Pao. "It is not focused primarily on the benefits received or the blessed condition of a person; instead, *God is the center* of thanksgiving."[22]

It is virtually impossible for an ungrateful Christian to be a worshiping Christian. And it is almost impossible for a grateful, thankful Christian to *not* be a worshiping Christian.

Intercession

Gratitude is crucial to proper intercession. Several years ago I took a walk to spend some time praying for several personal needs. I began to pray about a close relative's problems. I had been praying about this subject for several weeks, but God had not answered, and I was becoming fearful and frustrated. It dawned on me that something was wrong—I was not supposed to feel frustrated and stressed while interceding. What was going on? The next day I read Paul's words in Philippians 4:4–7, and everything changed.

> Rejoice in the Lord always; again I will say, Rejoice. Let your reasonableness be known to everyone. The Lord is at hand; do not be anxious about anything, but in everything by prayer and supplication with thanksgiving let your requests be made known to God. And the peace of God, which surpasses all understanding, will guard your hearts and your minds in Christ Jesus.

Paul's exhortation helped me see what I now call the prayer sandwich. In the middle is the meat, what you are asking God to do. On top is the bread of "rejoicing in the Lord always." For emphasis Paul repeats the command, "Again I will say, Rejoice." On the bottom is the second slice of bread—"with thanksgiving."

In other words, a believer who is *thankful* because God knows how and when to give the perfect answer at the perfect time will also *not be anxious about anything* and will know *the peace of God, which surpasses all understanding*. They will know this peace even when interceding for horrendous problems that God does not seem to be answering the way they want.

After reading this text, I returned to interceding for my relative, but now the burden was lifted. The stress and anxiety were gone. Indeed, thanksgiving during intercession "becomes an act of submission when the performance of such an act is not aimed at coercing God to act, but is a way to acknowledge him to be Lord of all."[23] A heart disciplined by thanksgiving will be effective at intercession.

Fear of the Future

Gratitude helps us overcome fear of the future. Many people live in constant dread of the future. They remember how a relative died a long, painful death and assume it will happen to them, too. They hear stories about the Great Depression and wonder how they would survive a similar experience. They read about a teen killed in a car accident and are sure it will happen to someone they love.

But thanksgiving conquers dread of the future. It doesn't deny that difficulties might come. As we have seen, sometimes great trials do come to those who follow Christ. We don't wish away the possibility of difficulties with denial. Instead, far better than a fantasy life, we can conquer fear of the future with faith. Because the Christian believes that God is both sovereign and good, he or she can look to the future with thanksgiving and gratitude. We really do trust in God's goodness. We fervently believe that God is in charge of future problems, and that he has designed them all for our good.

This is how a heart of gratitude conquers dread of the future.

Relationships

Gratitude is necessary for healthy relationships. Thankful people are uniquely equipped to resolve relational problems, especially when people have not lived up to their expectations or let them down in some significant way.

Immature children, selfish mates, irritating friends, unbelieving relatives, and persecuting work associates are the common experience of men and women living in a fallen world. Grateful Christians have learned to be thankful for what people can give, not what they cannot.

Think of the church at Corinth. They had major issues. A man in the church was practicing incest. The membership was divided over Paul, Apollos, and Cephas. People were getting drunk at communion. Some even denied the resurrection. Paul had every reason to be angry, resentful, and disappointed. But notice how he starts his letter.

> I give *thanks* to my God always for you because of the grace of God that was given you in Christ Jesus, that in every way you were enriched in him in all speech and all knowledge—even as the testimony about Christ was confirmed among you—so that you are not lacking in any spiritual gift, as you wait for the revealing of our Lord Jesus Christ (1 Corinthians 1:4–7).

Thanksgiving! Why would Paul be thankful? Here is the reason. Although the church was immature, sinful, and struggling with all kinds of problems, there was nevertheless a church where, in the light of God's justice, there should not have been one. None of us deserves to participate in a church. There will be no churches in hell. Therefore, Paul is grateful for God's unmerited favor. With that attitude as a foundation he searches for something to be thankful for and comes up with three things—speech, knowledge, and spiritual gifts. In the same way, a heart overflowing with gratitude equips us to work through difficult relationships. It doesn't minimize people's problems or fail to be critical when necessary, but it sees every relationship from the perspective of what it deserves.

I have never had a couple come to me for marriage counseling that was practicing the discipline of gratitude for each other. Just the opposite. They are always complaining and grumbling. Underneath their words is the assumption, *I deserve better than I am getting*. "She doesn't serve me." "He doesn't meet my needs." "She always does _____."

But thankful people see problem relationships as a glass half-full, not half-empty. Those around them sense this. They feel their hope and their affection. They trust them. We go to thankful people with our problems.

This is especially true with our children, our spouses, our parents, the pastor who is less than perfect, and that boss at work who has a volcanic temper and is in an adulterous relationship with a woman in the office.

Joy

Gratitude is the secret of spiritual joy. In the Bible, thanksgiving is a big subject, and the apostle Paul is its greatest advocate. New Testament scholar P.T. O'Brien observes that "Paul mentions the subject of thanksgiving in his letters more often, line for line, than any other Hellenistic author, pagan or Christian."[24] Paul's letters literally bristle with exhortations to a grateful, thankful way of life.

Thanksgiving makes people happy. "Over time," notes Nancy Leigh DeMoss, "choosing gratitude means *choosing joy*."[25] That is because a thankful heart is a cheerful heart. As we saw earlier in this chapter, it is a sign of contentment. Its fruits are increasing humility, meekness, and contentment. A grateful, thankful heart points to a deep deposit of true and living faith.

In a *Christianity Today* article, Mollie Hemingway writes,

> Studies show that grateful people are happier and more satisfied with their lives and social relationships. They are more forgiving and supportive than those who are ungrateful. They are less depressed, stressed, envious, and anxious. In fact, high levels of gratitude explain more about psychological well-being than 30 of the most commonly studied personality traits, according to two recent studies published in the journal *Personality and Individual Differences*.[26]

"Gratitude," notes the *Tyndale Bible Dictionary,* "is a *joyful* commitment of one's personality to God."[27]

Why are grateful people happy?

First, thankful people are in contact with reality. They see themselves crucified with Christ. They have shed the pretensions of personal greatness that ultimately make us miserable. They have quit trying to be "somebody." They are at rest with their creaturehood, their finiteness, and the knowledge of what they deserve. They live by God's unmerited favor and delight to have it that way. In other words, they are at rest with themselves and with God.

Second, thankful people are like Paul. They have learned, whatever their situation, to be content (Philippians 4:11). They know that they are not in control of their lives. God is. They know he is sovereign and good and completely committed to their welfare, so they trust him. When trouble comes they are grateful. When monotony comes they are thankful. When plenty and abundance come they overflow with thanksgiving. They are increasingly content, and contented people are happy people.

✵ ✵ ✵

My closing task in this book is to motivate you. I want to leave you with a clear and inspiring vision that will help compel you, by God's grace, to commit to changing in this area. I pray these words have their intended effect.

✵ ✵ ✵

In the final analysis, a grateful heart is the by-product of many choices. A heart overflowing with gratitude is one that has disciplined itself to respond to life's routines—toasted bread, coffee, marriage, insurance, civil government, technology, transportation, etc.—with a habit of thankfulness. Grateful people take nothing for granted. They have disciplined their hearts to respond to life's unexpected problems and joys with gratitude.

Whatever your history—whatever struggles you have had with grumbling, complaining, and self-pity—you can learn to live with biblical gratitude. The process is not complicated. A heart welling over with genuine thanksgiving—despite challenging circumstances—can be yours. This is not my promise. It's God's promise. God wants us to be joyful in him because of the finished work of Jesus Christ. Speak words of gratitude to God. Speak them in your mind, speak them in your heart, speak them with your mouth. The daily practice of specific gratitude is essential—indeed, it is necessary—to our joy.

Can I encourage you to pursue this discipline? It is a lifestyle worth fighting for every day. A grateful heart flows from the conviction that God is both infinitely sovereign and absolutely good, and therefore in every circumstance he is accomplishing what is best for me. The ultimate proof and ground for this conviction is the fact that God redeemed me through the cross of Christ, when all I should have received from him was well-deserved eternal condemnation. Even at this moment I deserve hell, but I am getting heaven at Christ's expense.

When you see the simple, biblical truth of all this, everything becomes a subject for gratitude and thanksgiving. Words of thanks conquer our complaining, grumbling, and self-pity. They glorify God and delight our hearts.

A grateful heart is the secret of spiritual joy. And who doesn't want that?

Endnotes

1. Margaret Visser, *The Gift of Thanks* (New York: Houghton, Mifflin, Harcourt, 2008), 8.

2. Allen C. Myers, *The Eerdmans Bible Dictionary* (Grand Rapids: Eerdmans, 1987), 996.

3. Michael Green, *The Message of Matthew : The Kingdom of Heaven* (Downers Grove: Inter-Varsity Press, 2000), 105.

4. Brian H. Edwards, *God's Outlaw: The Story of William Tyndale and the English Bible* (Evangelical Press: Darlington, 1976), 113.

5. S. Pearce Carey, *William Carey* (London: Wakeman Trust, 1923), 285.

6. Ibid., 286.

7. "1755 Lisbon Earthquake," *Wikipedia*, accessed October 19, 2015, https://en.wikipedia.org/wiki/1755_Lisbon_earthquake.

8. John Frame, *Doctrine of God* (Phillipsburg: P&R, 2002), Chapter 3, "The Lordship Attributes: Control." Also see an extensive treatment of the various Scriptures relating to God's sovereignty in Frame's *Systematic Theology* (Phillipsburg: P&R, 2013), Chapter 8, "The Providence of God."

9. Jerry Bridges, *Trusting God Even When Life Hurts*, (Colorado Springs: NavPress, 2008), 35.

10. Here are a few places where all or part of Exodus 34:6–7 are repeated in whole or part. Numbers 14:18; 2 Chronicles 30:9; Nehemiah 9:17; Psalm 86:15; 103:8; 111:4; 112:4; 116:5; 145:8; Joel 2:13; Jonah 4:2; and Nahum 1:3.

11. Isaiah 53:1–10; Psalm 22:1,8,16,18; John 19:24, 28, 36; Psalm 69:4,9, 21–22; Psalm 41:9; Matthew 21:4–5; Zechariah 11:13; Luke 24:44; and John 18:8–9.

12. Liz Mantell, "Millions in Bangladesh face slow poisoning from arsenic-contaminated water," December 2, 1998, *World Socialist Website*, accessed October 19, 2015, http://www.wsws.org/en/articles/1998/12/bang-d02.html.

13. Richard Smith, "Self Pity Will Destroy You," June 24, 2004, BMJ.com, accessed October 19, 2015, http://bmj.bmjjournals.com/cgi/content/full/328/7455/0-g.

14. Paul Mizzi, "The Bitter Fruits of Self Pity," *Truth For Today*, accessed October 19, 2015, http://www.tecmalta.org/tft293.htm.

15. Jay Adams, "Self Pity," *Journal of Biblical Counseling*, 9:4, (1989).

16. Nancy Leigh DeMoss, *Choosing Gratitude* (Chicago: Moody, 2009), 80.
17. William P. Farley, *Gospel Powered Humility* (Phillipsburg: P&R, 2012).
18. David Pao, *Thanksgiving* (Leicester: Apollos, 2002), 35, italics mine.
19. Ibid., 36.
20. DeMoss, *Choosing Gratitude*, 82.
21. George Marsden, *Jonathan Edwards* (New Haven: Yale, 2003), 361, italics mine.
22. Pao, *Thanksgiving*, 28–29, italics mine.
23. Pao, *Thanksgiving*, 37.
24. Peter O'Brien, "Benediction, Blessing, Doxology, Thanksgiving," *Dictionary of Paul and His Letters*, edited by Gerald F. Hawthorne, Ralph P. Martin, and Daniel G. Reid (Downers Grove, IVP, 1993), 69.
25. DeMoss, *Choosing Gratitude*, 17, Italics mine.
26. Mollie Ziegler Hemingway, "The Parent of all Virtues," *Christianity Today*, November 22, 2010, Online article.
27. Walter A. Elwell and Philip Wesley Comfort, *Tyndale Bible Dictionary* (Wheaton: Tyndale House Publishers, 2001), 551.

Author

Bill Farley was converted to Christ while doing graduate studies at Gonzaga University in 1971. He worked for 25 years in the business world before retiring from his business in 1999 to pursue full-time ministry. In 2002 he became the senior pastor of Grace Christian Fellowship in Spokane, Washington. He is the author of numner books, including Gospel Powered Humility (P&R Sept 2011) and Hidden in the Gospel (P&R Feb 2014). Bill and his wife, Judy, live in Spokane, Washington. They have five children and twenty grandchildren.

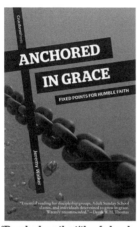

Anchored in Grace
Fixed Truths for Humble Faith

by Jeremy Walker

Clear truths from Scripture...

**Central. Humbling. Saving.
Comforting. God-glorifying.**

Get Anchored.

*86 pages
bit.ly/ANCHRD*

"Rarely does the title of a book so clearly represent its contents as does this one. With brevity and precision, Jeremy Walker sets forth God's work of salvation in the believer from beginning to end. In a day when there is so much confusion regarding even the most fundamental truths of redemption, this concise yet comprehensive work is a clear beacon of light to guide the seeker and to instruct and comfort the believer."
Paul David Washer, Director, HeartCry Missionary Society

"As a pastor, I am always looking for a book that is brief, simple, and biblical in its presentation of the God-exalting doctrines of grace to put into the hands of believers. I think my search is now over!"
Conrad Mbewe, African Christian University, Lusaka, Zambia

"Crisp, clear, concise, and biblical, Walker's book offers up the doctrines of God's grace in a manner persuasive to the mind and powerful to the heart."
Dr. Joel R. Beeke, Pres., Puritan Reformed Theological Seminary

"A sure-footed journey...a trusted guide. Reading this book will both thrill and convict, challenge and confirm. Essential reading for discipleship groups, Adult Sunday School classes, and individuals determined to grow in grace. Warmly recommended."
Derek W. H. Thomas, Professor, Reformed Theological Seminary

Torn to Heal
God's Good Purpose in Suffering

by Mike Leake

**Recieve comfort for today.
Be prepared to for tomorrow.**

*87 pages
Learn more at bit.ly/TORN2H*

"The most concise, readable, and helpful theology of suffering I've
come across. The content, length, and tone is just perfect for those
who are in the furnace of affliction screaming 'Why?'"
Dr. David Murray, Puritan Reformed Theological Seminary

"Mike Leake has taken the ugliness of suffering, turned it over in his
capable hands, and shown God's goodness and faithfulness in the
midst. More than simple encouragement, it is a handbook of scrip-
tural truths about Who God is and how He sustains."
Lore Ferguson writes for Gospel Coalition, CBMW, and more

"A gospel-driven path between dualism that acts as if God has lost
control of his world and fatalism/stoicism that tries to bury pain
beneath emotionless acceptance of whatever happens. The result is
a brief but potent primer on the purpose of suffering."
Timothy Paul Jones, Southern Baptist Theological Seminary

"Explores God's redemptive purposes in human suffering in a concise,
biblical and authentic way. Mike shuns cliches and platitudes to help
the reader put life's hardships into divine perspective and to endure
in Christ's strength. It is a must-read for Christians in distress."
Dave Miller, Second Vice-President, Southern Baptist Convention

TORN TO HEAL, Chapter 1 Excerpt

(Much smaller type than usual!)

THE PROMISE AND THE HOPE

No one ever told me that an undersized 10-year-old from a small midwestern town has basically no chance of growing up to become a professional athlete. If anyone had it wouldn't have mattered though, because it was my destiny. I was sure of it. And while it was nice that my mom and grandmother seemed to agree with me, that was nothing compared to the next name I put on the list.

Lou Brock.

Baseball Hall-of-Famer. Eighteen years in the majors. Lifetime .293 batting average. Destroyed Ty Cobb's stolen-base record. Lou Brock is a baseball god.

I was barely 10 when my uncles took me to some event where Brock was appearing. When it came time for questions I raised my hand. This just seemed like a fun way to participate, but somehow Brock spotted the goofy little kid with glasses and picked me. He pointed right at me! I didn't even have a bad question in mind much less a brilliant one. In the silence, my brain racing, the crowd around me seemed to grow from hundreds to at least a million. I stumbled and stuttered and finally squeaked out a question: "What did it feel like to break a record?"

His answer was something about ghosts and them chasing you. I can't exactly remember because I was too busy checking to see if my pants were still dry. But when it came time for autographs, I do remember what he said. As I walked up towards him, probably looking more like a 7-year-old than a 10-year-old, he smiled and said, "Hey kid, maybe someday you'll break a record."

Mom, Grandma, and now Lou Brock. My list of supporters had just gone world-class. I was instantly infused with hope. Yeah! Maybe I can make it to the majors. Maybe I can be a professional baseball player and challenge Ricky Henderson for the stolen base record.

(Editor's Note: Mike Leake actually did make the major leagues as a pitcher for the Cincinnati Reds. The author hopes you will overlook the fact that this was a different Mike Leake.)

Of course Brock was just being nice to me, but his quip added fuel to the fire of my dreams. I took his words almost as a kind of promise—an authoritative baseball prophecy. And in my little-boy heart the flame of that promise burned bright and strong for a long time to come.

A promise from someone you trust can do that. It can shape your identity for years, or even a lifetime.

A God of Huge Promises

God makes promises too, from Genesis to Revelation. The Christian faith hangs on those promises, and while the promise God made to Abraham was not the first divine promise recorded in Scripture, it was the first to shape the identity of an entire people for thousands of years. In fact the story of Abraham "dominates the book of Genesis and casts a shadow which extends across the whole Bible."[1] God's promise to Abram (later renamed Abraham) in Genesis 12:1-3 may very well be "the text the rest of the Bible expounds."[2] This particular promise would go on to shape the history, not merely of a nation, but of the entire world.

> Now the LORD said to Abram, "Go from your country and your kindred and your father's house to the land that I will show you. And I will make of you a great nation, and I will bless you and make your name great, so that you will be a blessing. I will bless those who bless you, and him who dishonors you I will curse, and in you all the families of the earth shall be blessed." (Genesis 12:1-3)

This promise to Abram stands in stark contrast to the brokenness that emerges in the Bible beginning in Genesis chapter 3. Then for the next eight chapters the reader encounters the fallen world with which we are all too familiar. Death, murder, pain, and rebellion smatter the pages as a pervasive corruption spreads throughout

God's good creation. This is the backdrop against which the shocking declaration of Genesis 12:1-3 is cast, telling us that in the midst of all this brokenness, blessing will appear. As Christopher Wright has aptly noted:

> The call of Abraham is the beginning of God's answer to the evil of human hearts, the strife of nations, and the groaning of brokenness of his whole creation. It is the beginning of the mission of God and the mission of God's people.[3]

Through Abraham and his seed all the nations would be blessed. He and his innumerable seed would possess the land of promise forever and, as a friend of God, Abraham's name would be great.

This promise to Abram, though, is not new. It looks back to the pre-fall Edenic state of mankind. This formation of a new nation is really the reformation of a new humanity.[4] The Lord, through Abraham and his seed, is fulfilling God's original promise that the seed of the woman will crush the serpent (Genesis 3:15). Our calling as divine representatives and image-reflectors to rule, rest, and be in relationship would somehow be restored through the offspring of this old man named Abram.

Impossible Odds

God's promises often seem shocking to us. They are God-sized promises, seldom anything we could hope to accomplish on our own. Naturally they can seem outlandish, even impossible.

God promises Abraham that his offspring will be a blessing to the whole world. But God does not make this promise when Abraham is 25 and with a fertile wife. No, he waits until Abraham is childless and pushing the century mark. He waits until the child-bearing days of Abraham's wife, Sarah, are so long past that the very idea of her becoming pregnant is laughable.

That's the kind of promise God makes—the kind that's very hard to believe.

Read the first 2 chapters free: www.bit.ly/TORN2H

Good News About Satan
A Gospel Look at Spiritual Warfare

by Bob Bevington
Foreword by Jerry Bridges

The world, the flesh...the Devil and his demons. How do they work together against us?

Learn to recognize and resist the enemy in the power of the gopel.

108 pages
bit.ly/SATANLOSES

"Spiritual warfare is certainly an important biblical topic; from one perspective it is the central topic of the whole Bible. So it's important that believers get sober and reliable guidance on the subject. Bob Bevington's book is one of the most helpful. His book is reliable, biblical, and practical. It is easy to understand and challenges our spiritual complacency."
Dr. John M. Frame, Reformed Theological Seminary

"This is the best book I have ever read on this subject. I simply could not put it down. It is both highly Christ-centered and very practical, having the wonderful effect of focusing the reader's attention directly on Jesus while at the same time providing much useful help in the believer's battle against the enemy."
Mike Cleveland, Founder and President, Setting Captives Free

"Filled with biblical reconnaissance and helpful insights for the conduct of spiritual warfare... a stimulating analysis of the biblical data, drawing boundaries between the factual and fanciful, and grounding the reader firmly on the gospel of Jesus Christ."
Stanley Gale, author, What is Spiritual Warfare?

"Read this book, prepare for battle, and rejoice in the victory that has been won and the glory that will shine more brightly."
Justin Taylor, co-author, The Final Days of Jesus

The Two Fears
Tremble Before God Alone

by Chris Poblete

**You can fear God...
or everything else.**

**Only one fear brings life and hope,
wisdom and joy.**

Fear wisely.

92 pages   bit.ly/2Fears

"We are too scared. And we aren't scared enough. Reading this book
   will prompt you to seek in your own life the biblical tension between
   'fear not' and 'fear God.'"
   Russell D. Moore, Dean, Southern Baptist Theological Seminary

"An importantly counter-cultural book, moving us beyond a
   homeboy God we could fist-bump to a holy God we can worship.
   The Two Fears helps us recover a biblical fear of God and all the awe,
   repentance, and freedom from self-centered fears that go with it. An
   awesome resource!"
   Dr. Thaddeus Williams, professor, Biola University

"In this practical and very readable book, Chris Poblete shows how
   both the absence of true fear and the presence of 'unholy [false] fear'
   stem from an absence of a knowledge of the awesome God of the
   Bible, and that, in meeting him, we discover the real dimensions of
   creational existence and the wonderful benefits of living in fear and
   deep respect before him, freed from the '[false] fear of men.'"
   ***Peter Jones, Ph.D., TruthXchange; Scholar-in-Residence and
   Adjunct Professor, Westminster Seminary in California***

"I commend this book to you: it will fuel your worship and empower
   your discipleship."
   Gabe Tribbett, Christ's Covenant Church, Winona Lake, IA

Inductive Bible Studies for Women by Keri Folmar

JOY! – A Bible Study
on Philippians
for Women

bit.ly/JoyStudy

GRACE: A Bible
Study on Ephesians
for Women

bit.ly/GraceStudy

FAITH: A Bible
Study on James
for Women

bit.ly/FaithStudy

"It is hard to imagine a better inductive Bible Study tool."
–Diane Schreiner

Keri's studies have been endorsed by...

Kathleen Nielson is author of the *Living Word Bible Studies*; Director
of Women's Initiatives, The Gospel Coalition; and wife of Niel,
who served as President of Covenant College from 2002 to 2012.

Diane Schreiner – wife of professor, author, and pastor Tom Schreiner,
and mother of four grown children – has led women's Bible
studies for more than 20 years.

Connie Dever is author of *The Praise Factory* children's ministry
curriculum and wife of Pastor Mark Dever, President of 9 Marks
Ministries.

Kristie Anyabwile, holds a history degree from NC State University,
and is married to Thabiti, currently a church planter in Washington, D.C., and a Council Member for The Gospel
Coalition.

Gloria Furman is a pastor's wife in the Middle East and author of
Glimpses of Grace and *Treasuring Christ When Your Hands Are Full*.